CASTLES of EUROPE

Carlos Paluzie de Lescazes

CRESCENT BOOKS - NEW YORK

CASTLES
of
EUROPE

Copyright © 1982 by E.G.C. S.A.
Hurtado, 29 - BARCELONA - SPAIN

All rights reserved.
First English language edition published by E.G.C. S.A.
This edition is published by Crescent Books.
Distributed by Crown Publishers Inc.
h g f e d c b a

Printed in Spain
By C.E.D.A.G, S.A.
San Juan Despí - BARCELONA - SPAIN
Management: S. SABATER CASAS
Coordination: JUAN L. LLADÓ LLEÓ
Textbook and realization: Carlos Paluzie de Lescazes
Photographs: Firo Foto - Barcelona
Lay-outs: Mercedes Broto
Colour separations: Artis, S.A.
Photocomposition: Typex, S.A.
Translation and adaptation: Daniel Anthony Marion

Library of Congress Cataloging in Publication Data:
De Lescazes Carlos Paluzle
Castles of Europe
D 910.5.R67 728.8'1 81-15167
ISBN 0-517-36200-7 AACR2

SOURCE OF PICTURES.   All pictures researched and compiled by Firo-Foto Archivo Fotográfico (Barcelona)

A.G.E. FotoStock.   G. Baronc. 70, D.A. Duncan. 44-45, Gutierrez. 42, V. Guy: 31; J.W. Kingshott: 41; P. Kormetzki: 74; F. Maden: 65; Mauritius: 116-117; Picture Point: 125; R. Pouplana: 72, 124; H. Schmied: 125; W. Wilke: 19, 56-57, 64; M. Wilson: 73.

AUNE Kunstforlag: 34. 35.

FIRO-FOTO Archivo: A. Band: 43 (top), 46 (top), 49, 50 (2); J. & J. Blassi: 127 (bottom); Robert Everts: 2-3, 7 (2), 8 (2), 9 (2), 13, 14 (2), 16-17, 27 (bottom), 28-29, 31, 37, 48, 52, 59, 60, 61 (2), 62, 63, 66-67, 71 (top left), 75, 76-77, 78, 79, 81 (2), 82-83, 84, 86, 87, 88 (2), 89, 90, 92-93, 96, 98, 103 (2), 104, 105, 106-107, 109 (left), 110, 111, 112 (top right), 112 (bottom), 126; S. Fiore: 23 (left), 24-25 (4), 36, 46 (bottom), 108 (bottom), 112 (top left), 114, 115, 127 (top) and back-cover; J. Griera: 95; J. Gumí: 23 (right); P. Koch: 27 (top), 91; P. Newark: 10, 11, 20, 21 (2), 22, 26; P. Nin: 85; Nordisk Pressefoto: 30, 32; F. Pérez-Catalá: 122; R. Pouplana: 121; S. Prato: 12, 71 (top right) 71 (bottom), 94, 97, 108 (top), 113: Pressfoto Agency: 33 (2).

SALMER Archivo: 43 (bottom), 47, 53, 54, 55, 80.

Courtesy of The Bulgarian Embassy in Spain: 118, 119, 120.

Introduction

The purpose of this book is to give a general idea of the importance of castles in the Middle Ages and the way of life that developed in and around them.

The social structures of the Middle Ages developed out of feudalism, a social and political system which came into being with the disintegration of the Carolingian Empire. Its growth during the 9th and 10th centuries was precipitated by the conditions under which people lived during the Dark Ages. Feudalism spread from its birthplace in France to other European countries, and in particular to Germany, Italy, England and northern Spain.

The end of the first millennium was one of the most tragic eras in Western European history; danger was widespread and established values had disappeared along with the last vestiges of the Carolingian Renaissance. From all corners of Europe, invasions by Vikings, Arabs and Hungarians had wrought havoc and destroyed what remained of civilization. Rulers had little power and all forms of authority were undermined. The centres of defence became the fortified manors and castles ruled over by the local lords, which became strongholds where the individual could find relative refuge.

The roots of feudalism lay in the Low Roman Empire, fostered by the proliferation of large estates (*latifundia*) that had also been characteristic of the Roman Empire. The new class of powerful landowners usurped attributes which today belong to the State and enforced strong ties and dependence. This gave rise to a social system whereby lords became rulers and which was subsequently to merge with a new social order brought about by the spread of fiefs.

Fiefs had their origin in the fusion of two institutions: rights to the use of land and vassalage. The right to land represented the privilege of using it during the lifetime of the individual to whom the right was granted; vassalage meant the swearing of allegiance and rendering of services by one man to another in exchange for protection. The bond represented dependence and submission, and it was directly related to the strength of the castle and its lord. Both parties owed one another counsel and help, which was usually in the form of armed service, limited to forty days. Vassals were also called on to give up a number of days each year in defence of the local baron's castle.

5

When there was an attack, the people in the surrounding area took refuge in the castle, and the castle's church became the parish church. The lands they tilled belonged to the lord of the castle and the position of the peasants was that of serfs. What had once been nascent national groupings became divided and subdivided into miniscule local entities centered on an infinity of castles, which served as their nucleus and reason for existence. Fiefs held by the most powerful ruling families became hereditary and accumulated into vast estates which were independent of the throne for all practical purposes unless they vied with it for local hegemony. The vital role of the castle during these times was to represent a bulwark of defence in the incessant quarrels which arose in the small, semi-autonomous communities.

Out of the semi-anarchy, arose social structures and laws based on verbal contract. A pyramidal social structure developed, with the king at the pinnacle. The chain of authority extended from the king to the nobles loyal to him, from the nobles to the subjects loyal to them, and so on. Each unit was tied by the bond of homage stemming from vassalage, and the system was perpetuated by rites which were practised with utmost rigour.

Castle building was strictly regulated. Permission was granted only to the nobles and given only by the sovereign, who was also entitled to destroy castles erected without his consent. When this happened it often lead to war, and this instinct for independence on the part of the sovereign's barons led them to insurrection when he was away or at war.

The feudal system established itself as the social order in all countries, and covered not only territorial holdings but also public offices and affairs of state. Even the minting of money became hereditary. Any concept of public authority was undermined by the immunity of the barons within their own domains. They had their own officials and exercised jurisdiction over their vassals until it was impossible to imposeany form of state authority over the population at large.

The way the throne regained power was by establishing centralised administration, extending its land holdings, by usurpation and by war. With the growth of central power, feudalism began to decline and the power of the barons was checked.

The castles, fortresses and palaces included in this book are not necessarily the most important nor the best known. Other books have discussed the most important castles. The ones chosen represent a heterogeneous grouping characteristic of the development and diversity of military architecture. A small and unknown castle or palace is often more significant than a famous showpiece, because it may have played an important role at a particular time in history.

Carlos Paluzie de Lescazes

ORIGINS AND HISTORY

What is a castle? The first picture that comes to mind is of an enclosure set on high ground and fortified against attack. This holds true until the 15th century, when the castle was no longer needed as a military bastion in the times of greater peace, and the military stronghold gave way to the palace.

The first military strongholds were built by primitive man, as a

Lorca.

protection against wild animals and other men. They were generally sited on an elevated spot, such as plateaus surrounded by cliffs, or strategically placed near rivers, river confluences or crossroads. As the tribes used these early castles more and more to live in, and as storehouses for food, goods and booty, the original small military enclosures grew into large structures, which also housed temples where primitive man worshipped. As the population grew, houses were built beyond the boundaries and down the side of the hill, though still in the shadow and under the protection of the fortress (*acropolis*).

The *pax romana* (Roman peace) had a lasting influence on military organization in much of Europe. Order was maintained by a system of border posts. These became permanent camps, from which many of the European cities sprang. The *castellum* (castle), adapted to the land on which it was built, emerged to protect the roads, coasts, river crossings and populations. It consisted of a square, wooden tower several storeys high and crowned

LORCA (Spain)
Built in the 13th century on the site of an existing Moorish fortress, Lorca Castle has sturdy walls made of compact earth mixed with stones.

SAUMUR (France)
Several fortresses preceded the present palace on its site in the Loire Valley. Built during the 15th and 16th centuries, the palace has minimal military characteristics. Note the wide windows and the ornamental chimneys and turrets.

WOODEN TOWER
Built onto an artificial elevation. It is surrounded by a moat and a wooden stockade and was originally the focal point of the castle.

Saumur.

with an upper terrace of battlements. There were strong walls or stockades of tree trunks, usually surrounded by a moat.

In its own country, the Roman villa was unfortified and the countryside was at peace. The landowner used it as a residence more than anything else, and as a farm, surrounded by storehouses and outbuildings for guests, cattle and slaves. The traditions of the early farmers were observed by later Roman citizens, who no longer used the villas for cultivation or farming. The citizen lived at peace within a countryside whose inhabitants had been subdued and thoroughly Romanized, and he had no need to reinforce his home against armed attack.

The Low Roman Empire was the beginning of a new era. The decline of the institutions and military collapse of Rome brought about far-reaching changes. The Roman patricians abandoned their villas and took refuge in the towns, which began to be fortified. The Teutons invaded, conquering the lands once held by the Roman Empire and building fortresses to defend their territories against subsequent warring barbarians. Wars covered the old Empire; quarrels broke out between factions, between tribes and between monarchs; despite resistance from the Romanized population, there was a new surge of invasions in the 9th and 10th centuries. The times brought forth new needs. Defence was no longer concentrated on the Empire's old borders but spread throughout the lands it had once protected, and the first medieval castles appeared.

PEÑARANDA de DUERO (Spain)
A typical fortress of the 15th century, in which military elements predominate over the residential ones. It was built on high ground upon the remains of an 11th century fortress.

CAERNARVON (England)
A majestic royal palace built on the peninsula formed by the confluence of the Seiont and Menai rivers. It occupies the site of an earlier structure built by Hugo of Lupus, one of the Norman followers of William the Conqueror.

Peñaranda de Duero.

Caernarvon.

Atienza.

Torrelobatón.

The two military nuclei that were to develop over a period of nearly 800 years were the fortress and the castle. Fortresses were large buildings of fortified enclosures used to house a permanent garrison and to defend a particular site and its surroundings. They were generally controlled by kings or great princes. The term castle covers strong buildings, strategically sited and easily defended by a small garrison, whose first use was exclusively military, but which were later adapted to other purposes. Castles often became residences for the feudal lords.

Although the Teutons were an independent and warring people, with little feeling of nationhood, their castles present great variety, and the whims and personal tastes of the lords can be detected in their location and construction.

Later invaders, like the Vikings (later to become the Normans), had a different system of defence and formed a network of castles to defend their territory. They began to settle and build permanent structures by the 10th century. Their first forts were no more than camps surrounded by a wooden stockade and a moat, sufficient to protect men and loot. Although they sometimes used the old Roman *castri* (fortified camps), they quickly realised that to protect the territories that Charlemagne's successors had ceded them, they needed to create defence posts within a fortified system.

In the middle of the 10th century, the Normans moved from their forts and began to erect small stone castles built with great care, which were impressive at the time. Their basic plan was taken from that of earlier systems: a wall of stakes surrounded by a wide moat, and in the middle a fortified tower of several storeys, now often made of stone, also surrounded by a moat. The entrance to the tower, which was above ground level, could be reached only by ladder or by a bridge across the moat.

The kings of the Charlemagne era tended to guarantee their power by using hostages, by setting up a sound administration and by religious colonization. There are, however, clear references that they

FORTIFIED TOWER.
Built of mortar over a natural or artificial mound, surrounded by a moat and a stockade of earth or, later, of wood. Within the courtyard are several buildings, either attached to or embedded in the outer walls.

ATIENZA (Spain).
Keep built on a rough rocky platform and surrounded by a wall which takes in part of the rock. The small, angular turret belongs to a later date, when the 11th century building was restored.

TORRELOBATON (Spain).
Overlooking a small village at its foot, the present imposing fortress occupies the site of an earlier, 11th century citadel. The ground plan is an irregular square. The high walls and slender look-out posts mounted on three corners surround a double courtyard. The keep is over 100 ft and 3 storeys high.

Angevin.

ENGLISH CASTLE at the time of the Angevines.

1. *Drawbridge,* giving access over the moat to the main gate.

2. *Entrance,* usually protected by towers or, as here, forming a self-contained defensive unit resembling a miniature castle housed within the more spacious courtyard of the fortress.

3. *Main gate* — portcullis. This is an iron or wooden grating reinforced with straps which raised and lowered in grooves and hung from ropes or chains, for this purpose.

4. *Grated windows.* These are vertical slits or openings in the walls and towers which widen towards the base on the inside, to allow an archer room to sit and shoot or throw projectiles upon approaching enemy forces. With the advent of firearms, the base was widened and rounded, to accommodate artillery.

5. *Walk* along the inner width of the walls for the sentries, which connected the different parts of the castle.

6. *Parapet* or protective wall for the walkway, built into the main wall; also used to support the platform of the towers and sometimes incorporating grated windows for use by archers.

7. *Merlons* — alternating open and solid parts of the parapets, walls and towers, provided to give protection and to allow shooting.

8. *Machicolation galleries* — crowning towers and walls that widened the base of the walkways, with openings from underneath which permitted firing directly onto the heads of those beneath.

9. *Quarters* for soldiers, domestic animals, provisions and other elements related to life in the castle. Usually built of wood.

10. *Fortified tower,* also known as a tower of homage, keep or donjon. Centre of the castle and last bastion to which defenders retreated if the outer defences were breached; also residence of the lord and his closest vassals. Its name «homage» is because it was here that vassals swore their oath of allegiance.

11. *Postern* or small door used to enter or leave the castle secretly. It was almost always hidden, or at least well-concealed.

did build fortresses too: in 762, Charlemagne fortified Fronsac in Saxony; a garrison was installed in Sigiburg; and in 789, a castle was built in Hohbeck. But by and large, the Carolingians preferred, as the Romans had done, to create country residences and palaces. Yet by the middle of the 9th century, the chroniclers and notaries were writing charters which hailed the construction of castles as an event worth mentioning, brought about by invasion, internal turmoil, dynastic conflict and unrest amongst the barons. In the Iberian Peninsula, both Arabs and Christians defended the fluctuating frontiers by building large fortresses and castles. The Arab chroniclers called the area that would later become the nucleus of Spanish unity, Castilla (land of castles). In 915, the lords of the Luxembourg-Tréveris region covered its mountains with castles, from which sprung Esch-sur-Sure and Luxembourg.

At the centre of the enclosure, there were generally a chapel, soldiers' quarters, granaries, and small structures such as the mill and oven. The open ground within the enclosure was used for cattle or gave shelter to serfs who, in exchange for their feudal services, were entitled to claim protection.

The barons were an independent breed and showed little inclination for loyalty to any superior, and particularly to the king. Their constant rebellions forced kings and princes to find ways of establishing control over them and their castles and convert them into instruments of government.

Feudalism was fully established around the middle of the 12th century. Around each fortress would be a constellation of castles, generally within 15 miles but occasionally, in heavily sub-divided castellanies, within only 6 to 9 miles. Now converted to religious and economic centres, the castles became the administrative hub of their fiefs. Sanctuaries would be built, partly within and partly outside the fortified enclosures, sometimes preceding the fortifications and sometimes coming afterwards. The new sanctuaries would

TOWER of LONDON. There has been a fortification on Tower Hill outside London since Roman times; rebuilt by King Alfred and reconstructed again by William the Conqueror, the building served as castle and palace. The illustration shows the Tower at the time of Henry VII (reigned from 1485 to 1509).

Tower of London.

Hohensalzburg.

generally be endowed with a grant of land, and from these concessions sprang satellite centres of power in the hands of the clergy, sited near the castles and around the church.

The castle gave protection to a host of economic functions. It became the site of commercial gatherings, markets and fairs, and these later developed into civil agglomerations. Provided that control always remained with him, the local baron was happy to foster every kind of commercial development Serfs were given mills, ovens and looms in return for their obligatory use and rent.

The need for a system of law to regulate local practice and to underpin the right of decree (the right to order, oblige and punish) gave rise to new administrative functions. A local judiciary sprang up, living either within the castle enclosure or in the neighbouring village, and it was the presence of these legal officers, servants, subordinate agents, notaries and scribes which differentiated the municipalities governed by local lords from the purely agricultural villages.

The restoration of power to the kings and princes and the weakening of the feudal lords, changed the organization of defence, as much on a local level as throughout the country. By the 14th and 15th centuries, the kings had seized monopoly control of military construction, although the Castillian lords tried to maintain local predominance in the face of the monarch's attempts to strengthen centralized rule via the feudal loyalty of the heads of the castles. Throughout Europe, the clash of interests gave rise to new types of fortification, as emphasis moved away from the castle as a defensive structure and shifted to the fortified house and manor. Communities of citizens began to fortify their villages and towns and stimulate the development of new arms, particularly artillery.

HOHENSALZBURG.
The Hohensalzburg fortress overlooks the Prince-Bishop city. It was built at the end of the 11th century by Archbishop Gebhard, an ally of the Pope, as a refuge against the nobles of southern Germany, supporters of the Emperor. The fortifications have been reinforced on several occasions.

Military Architecture

The principal defensive elements of a castle can be classified as follows:

a) Castles until the middle of the 11th century were rudimentary. They consisted of a moat defended by a talus, the whole protected by a wooden stockade or mud wall. At the centre was a mound on which the wooden tower was erected, where the ruling lord lived. The entrance to the tower was above ground level and reached by ladder.

Herm.

b) By the middle of the 13th century, the wooden stockade and towers had been replaced by a stone wall overlooked by towers at each corner. The central tower remained the residence of the ruling lord but was now built of stone and heavily fortified so as to withstand attack if the enclosure was penetrated.

c) The typical Romanesque castle of the period consisted of a keep, and an extensive outer area surrounded by a wall where the civilian population and their livestock could take refuge. This was known as the outer bailey or second courtyard. Between the keep and the outer area was a high inner wall, enclosing the chapel, the ceremonial hall and the palace. The area was called the inner bailey or basecourt. The Crusades adapted the castle to the Holy Land and the two most famous, Crac des Chevaliers and Sayun, influenced the development of castles in Europe. The keep (or tower of homage) ceased to be a passive element of defence and was converted to become the centre of

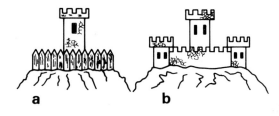

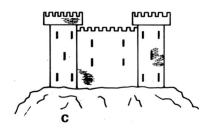

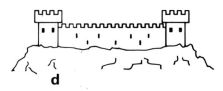

attack. It was still built within the enclosure but moved to the most vulnerable point in the defences and was given its own surrounding wall, known as the «shirt», which isolated it from all other buildings.

By the early 13th century, the French under Philip Augustus were the first to abandon this sprawl in favour of a smaller fortress. Far more obviously defensive structures, this generation of castles had high, thick walls, dominated as ever by the keep. The walk along the top of the walls allowed troops to move rapidly from one place to another.

HERM (France).
Located by the Herm River, a tributary of the Arriège, Herm Castle served as a refuge for bands of thieves in the 14th century. The keep is still standing, and the remains of the machicolation galleries are still visible.

DEVELOPMENT OF THE CASTLE.
a) tower defended by moat, talus and stockade; b) tower and stockade of stone, reinforced by towers at the corners; c) the castle's walls are higher, the better to defend the buildings that had sprung up within; d) citadel, built to withstand artillery; the walls are lower and bulwarked.

These stone castles were so expensive that they were within the reach of only kings and princes. Engineer-architects had to be brought in, skilled in technicalities like firing angles and possibilities for flanking movements. Each tower took

Sadaba.

nity of neighbours), by inhabitants (such as Arabs, Normans), or by their building plan (round, square or irregular).

The walls of the castles in the southern European countries, especially in Spain, Italy and Sicily, were

San Martín de Valdeiglesias.

SADABA (Spain).
Located to the north of the *cinco villas* (five villages) in Aragon, Sadaba was built at the beginning of the 13th century. The configuration is four-sided, with seven towers, four at the corners and three at the centre of the north, south and east façades. The tower on the south wall is so close to the one on the south-east corner that the one entry point, which was located between them, was well guarded. Sadaba is Cistercian in style, belonging to the period of transition between the heavy Romanesque castle, with its overpowering tower and sprawling walled courtyard, and the smaller and more easily and economically defended castle.

SAN MARTIN DE VALDEIGLESIAS (Spain).
Located on the site of an earlier fortress, San Martin de Valdeiglesias was built in the province of Madrid by Constable Alvaro de Luna in the 15th century. The groundplan is rectangular. Note the rounded openings in the towers, shaped to accommodate firearms.

OUTLINES OF TOWERS.
Towers were circular, semi-circular or square. The interior elevation was sometimes a straight wall or sometimes omitted, leaving the fortification open on the inside. If the tower were seized, the attackers were then vulnerable to assault by the defenders from the rest of the castle.

on the appearance of a miniature fort, and became a castle within a castle, entered via elbow-shaped access ways defended by lateral towers. The lord's quarters, freed of military use, became more comfortable and spacious.

d) The castles of the 14th, 15th and 16th centuries, adapted to withstand artillery by low walls fortified with bulwarks, are known as citadels. There are of several types, which are classified first by location (in plain countryside, on an elevation, or set within a town), then by the builder (royal, noble or commu-

built of adobe (unburnt brick dried in the sun), or of a cement made of pressed soil mixed with stones, which formed a hard, resistant surface. Bricks were another common material, or adobe covered with ashler, especially on corners of towers and walls.

The central element was always the tower, whether of wood or later of stone, which was built at the centre of the enclosure or later on the most vulnerable side or in the most inaccessible place, and which formed the last stronghold.

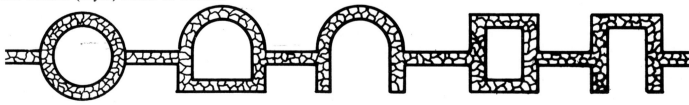

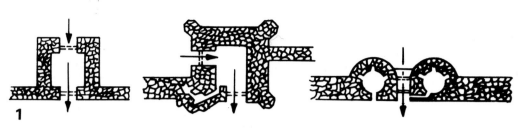

The Roman tower was square. The 10th and 11th century builders preferred a round tower for the central keep and used square towers for reinforcing corners of the outside walls. So that men in the outside square towers could continue to fight independently of the rest of the castle, these were set against the wall without forming a part of it. By the 12th century, the towers had begun to curve, under the Arab influence brought to Europe by the Crusades. By the 14th century, the square tower was back again because it was considered a more efficient way of flanking walls and led to better defence.

The 14th century tower was built with merlons (hollow spaces alternating with solid wall in the parapet, to facilitate firing), with machicolations (openings between the corbels which supported a projecting parapet, through which molten lead, stones etc were dropped upon assailants), or wooden scaffolding. Secure behind these parapets, the defenders could throw stones or boiling oil and the archers could shoot. This kind of tower was often open on the interior side so as to facilitate access and allow contact between the defenders and the garrison within the enclosure.

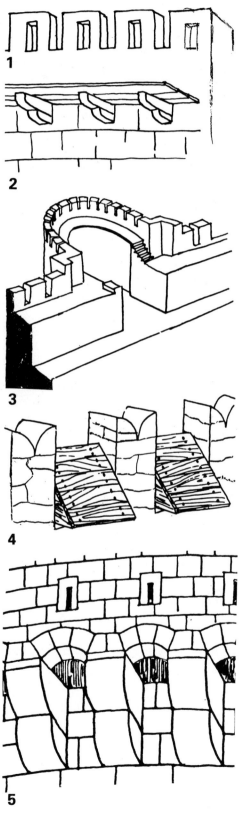

1. GATES.
The access gates to the castle were a vulnerable point, and were generally protected by towers on either side or by a miniature castle. Towers with an entrance at the base were generally square; the gate would be located either at the centre of a well, or on the side, so as to minimize damage from assault from battering rams.

2-3. PARAPET.
or breastwork— a wall protecting the interior walkway.

4. MERLONS.
Hollow spaces alternating with solid wall in the parapet, to facilitate firing by the defenders. Small windows were sometimes cut in the solid battlements. To protect the openings, wooden panels were occasionally used, which swung or were lifted into place.

5. MACHICOLATION GALLERIES.
Reinforcements of stone to the walkway or platform of the tower, which widened the base and which were pierced with firing holes.

ASCHAFFENBURG.
Powerful fortress belonging to the Archbishops of Maguncia, Aschaffenburg was built on the shores of the Main in the 16th century in Renaissance style, and surrounded by four defence towers.

1-2 FIRING CHAMBERS.
A small room or space in the walls behind small windows or embrasures where the defenders positioned themselves, or where the artillery pieces stood.

3. BUTTRESSES.
To deflect attackers' fire and to hinder the walls being scaled, towers were sometimes reinforced with buttresses, or sharp-pointed angular and vertical ridges.

There were problems in victualling the castles built on rock, on cliffs and mountains, unless there was at least a fountain or natural spring within the enclosure. Cisterns and large tanks had to be constructed with care, so as to avoid leaks or cracks, and to prevent contamination.

Barbican: an outer defence intended to protect any gate or other weak point of a fortification.

Gate or wall passage: heavily guarded and usually reinforced by one or two towers. The passage through the gate was not neccessarily straight, but sometimes angled or even zig-zag. At the head of the passage was a moat and a drawbridge. A door of heavy wood, reinforced with iron supports and locked with an iron bar, closed off the entrance. Overhead, either in front of the gate or behind, would be a vault pierced with small openings, to allow the gate to be guarded from above. In front of the gate was a **portcullis,** a heavy grill or iron panel which prevented access when lowered into place.

Linking the towers and enclosure walls was the **rampart** walk, which permitted the defenders to move freely from one vulnerable point to the next. The parapet was crowned with indented **battlements,** which were alternately solid and open, to allow both shooting and protection. The solid part of the battlements, known as **merlons,** could be flat or pointed. Between the battlements wooden panels, known as screens or shields, could be swung into place to cover the empty slots once a shot had been made. The **machicolations** were the crown of the towers and walls, forming a structure that widened the base of the rampart walk, but left holes and slits at floor level as openings for projectiles. In due course, the wooden scaffoldings above the parapet came to be replaced by stone.

Both towers and walls were pierced with openings and shooting chambers. The arrow holes in the

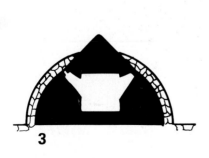

towers were straight slits or cross-shaped, while the heavy walls had openings cut into the thickness that formed a niche in which a defender could crouch and hurl projectiles. By the 14th century, they were using firearms.

The changes of the 13th and 14th centuries were to turn the keep into the lord's residence, and to enlarge the walled area still further so that it came to enclose three or four areas within their own walls and gates. At each wall, a successful attacker would lose more and more men before reaching the keep, the last stronghold. Another small wall came into use in the 14th century, known as the lining wall, which partially enclosed the base of the keep.

In common with the other castle towers, the keep often had a buttress, a vertical angular ledge that jutted out, reinforcing the tower and obstructing the approach of battle equipment.

By the end of the 15th century, the advent of artillery had caused a further change in castle architecture. Shooting niches in the tower walls were enlarged to allow them to hold medium caliber pieces of artillery. The walls were thicker than ever and sloped directly into the moat — a design created by Renaissance Italian engineers and later used by Vauban.

More chapels were built, beautifully sculptured. The lord's living quarters grew ever more spacious. Large and beautiful rooms were created with double or triple rows of narrow Gothic windows. A central patio was created within the palaces, enclosed by slender columns pointing to an arch and supporting an upper storey of galleries. The halls had painted wooden, coffered ceilings. The citadel itself became a massive fortification conforming to a pentagonal plan, with triangular bastions, wide moat and fortified glacis (the slope of the walls). Finally, the Renaissance style supplanted the Gothic.

The peak of Renaissance glory was the time when the absolute monarch emerged and his princes and nobles were in his shadow.

Fearful of rebellion, throughout Europe the monarchs ordered the destruction of their nobles' castles. It happened in Spain during the reign of Ferdinand and Isabel and in France during the reign of Louis VIII.

Because the old castles were no longer effective against modern artillery, some nobles gravitated to the royal courts, while others often moved out of their uncomfortable military establishments perched on strategic heights, and built new residences on flat ground, surrounded by comfort and parks. Amongst the most famous of this era are the Castles of the Loire in France. Maybe the most beautiful of these castles, many of them royal, are those of the Valois. Moats, towers and enclosures still existed, but they were used only as decorative elements. Finally, in the 17th and 18th centuries, the castle as such disappeared, now a palatial residence devoid of military use.

COCHEM (Germany). Virtually destroyed in 1689, Cochem Castle was reconstructed in its former style.

Cochem castle.

The castle at war. Defence and attack

The best defence of a stronghold was to guard against surprise attack. Watchdogs were used as much, if not more than sentry guards. A further precaution was to have sufficient stores of food and water for troops and any peasants taking refuge in the forecourt.

The following counsel is given by the Catalan Jaime Marquilles, in his *Comentaria susperusaticis*

Barchinone: «Where a castle is most vulnerable, there should stand watchdogs, geese and turkeys, and the art of sending carrier pigeons should be studied.» He advised the lord to keep, «salt, oil, string for crossbows, easy-to-store provisions like honey and acorns, large quantities of firewood, hemp, dry wool and rags for poulticing wounds». Keep no dice, checkers nor chess sets,

CATAPULT hurling incandescent material during a siege. Catapults were also used to fire burning torches, stones and balls of excrement.

Castle under Siege.

he advised, because these games encourage laziness and provoke fights. Keep books of chivalry and heroic deeds instead, as readings of this nature ought to delight and hearten the reader.

The Catalan said that the walls should be cemented with small, loose stones to stop ladders getting hold against the surface and to prevent soldiers getting a good grip if they tried to climb. A garden was highly recommended, stocked with cabbages and other vegetables, and let medicinal bags hang inside the enclosure. On the tops and the outsides of the walls, large bags of powder and dirt should be suspended which, when ripped apart, would spill their contents on the attackers and blind them. A supply of sulphur should be kept for burning devices and a supply of rawhides for putting out fires.

Nevertheless, the only real defence lay in repelling the attack of besiegers. If attackers tried to scale the walls, they would find them too high, and the surrounding moats too deep to cross. Rocks, burning resin and boiling oil would be dropped from the battlements and machicolated galleries, and every inhabitant, man, woman and child, was at the walls to destroy or burn the ladders.

Attacks began with a siege. The stronghold was surrounded, preventing either escape or the arrival of provisions or reinforcements. The besiegers built palisades (rows of strong, pointed wooden stakes) and military structures such as the wooden towers, which they rolled forward filled with men, preferrably before one of the gates.

The besiegers used machines and catapults. The defenders retaliated with their own catapults, which threw rocks from the towers and walls upon the attackers. Arrows and fire were thrown against the moving towers and battering rams. The attackers dug tunnels; the besieged dug countertunnels through which they tried to penetrate the first tunnel and repel attacking sappers.

After surrounding the stronghold, the walls and towers were

1

2

1. MODELS OF
    BATTERING RAM.
The ram's head model hit straight at the wall; the spearhead was pitched between joints and fissures to pry them loose. Rams were sometimes protected by a hut-like structure and mounted on wheels.

2. COUNTER-RAM.
The device was dropped on a battering ram as it was about to hit so as to avoid repetitive impact at the same point.

assaulted with scaling ladders and the moat was filled in. The attackers used catapults and battering rams to open a breach through which they could invade the first enclosure. If possible, the breach was made by one of the gates, so as to leave an entrance wide enough for a large number of men, or by tunnelling. The base of the walls and towers was undermined by trenching. Those within the castle made good these gaps in their defences with stockades of wood, but the attackers would fill the tunnels with loads of burning firewood, which weakened the walls and helped to topple them.

If repeated attack did not subdue the castle, and if the walls could not be breached, the next stage in a siege was to settle in round the stronghold and starve it out. Castles were never excessively provisioned at the best of times; with the courtyards filled with farmers and villagers from the surrounding areas, supplies had to be rationed from the outset. The defenders weakened for lack of food and water and, in time, were unable to hold out any longer.

Treason was another way of conquering a castle. There might always be someone within wishing to trade a safe conduct or a purse of gold in return for information on how to get in.

Equipment for a siege has a long history. Many of the devices used in the medieval attacks were similar to those used by the Roman legions, or even by the Greeks, whose mastery of the mechanical arts derived in turn from the Phoenecians and geometry.

The best known siege machinery were the catapult, the battering ram and the blunderbuss. These catapults could throw stones or burning barrels over distances of over 900 ft, and sometimes even putrefying carrion was tossed over the walls into the enclosure. Another weapon, more deadly in its precision, was the fixed crossbow which mounted on moving towers or used from the ground, had the force to break down the walls.

Military engineers probably accompanied the besieging army, because poor communications would have made it otherwise too difficult to gather them together when they

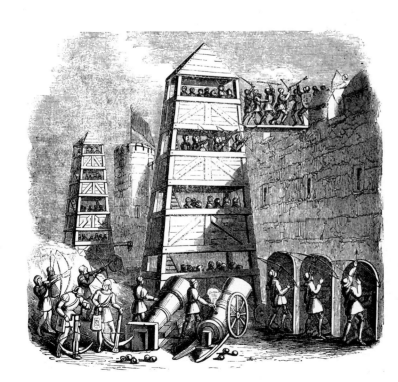

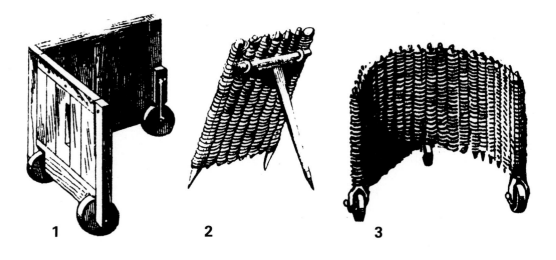

1   2   3

MANTLETS.
Worn by archers and crossbowmen for protection while giving covering fire to those pulling in the battering rams and portable towers or scaling the walls.

PORTUGUESE LAUNCHER.
Primitive cannon made of steel plates bent to form a tube and reinforced with heavy washers. Initially, they were used to fire solid stone balls. They had a relatively good firing range (excellent at the time).

CULVERIN.
From the 14th century. Cannon for heavy firing, reinforced with broad washers and held by ropes which controlled some of the firing backlash.

were needed. They built their engines on the spot, which put a premium on any forest areas near a castle, as a source of raw material.

The wooden towers would move in, several storeys high and crowded with shooting archers and crossbowmen, who jumped over the walled precinct or tried to penetrate the tower. Battering rams on wheels and protected with wooden shields, were pushed up against the walls to break them down.

A wooden shield on wheels, called a mantlet, protected the soldier as he advanced. The defenders used shields covered with damp skins to prevent their being set on fire.

Artillery was first used in the mid 14th century. There was artillery at Rouen in 1338 and at Florence in 1326. However, the first machines were erratic and frequently deadly to their gunners. Throwing arms, or catapults, were used alongside the

new weapons until the beginning of the 15th century, and castle architecture underwent few changes. The main pieces of artillery were bombards and mortars for firing at an angle and culverins for direct shots. Lighter, metallic cannonballs replaced the first, heavy stone balls in 1430, an invention of the Bureau brothers. Little by little, the artillery became more effective and its use changed. The first cannons were loaded through the breech. The method was abandoned in the 15th century, in favour of loading through the muzzle, because of gas leaks and wasted impact, and was used again only in the 19th century.

Portuguese Launcher.

Culverin.

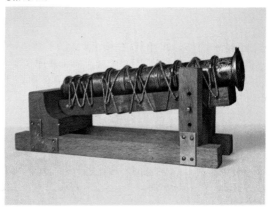

The castle as Home

Up till the middle of the 11th century, living in a castle was uncomfortable. The lord and his family generally lived in the upper storeys of the keep, and used partitioning to divide the space. His bodyguard lived on the ground floor with the cattle. Hygiene was non-existent. There were no sewage systems and no drains anywhere, whether in the castles, the villages or the towns, though there might be a latrine built into a castle wall and overhanging the ground outside. The mortality rate

The lady of the castle oversaw the kitchens and occupied herself with spinning and weaving. If a preaching or begging monk passed by, or a pilgrim, that was quite an event, and even more so if a juggler, a minstrel or a travelling fair turned up.

Nevertheless, by the end of the 12th century, when the great lordly castles began to be built, part residence and palace and part stronghold, some comforts were introduced and the way of life began to soften. The people no longer lived

SCENES FROM MEDIEVAL LIFE.
Italian painting depicting scenes from medieval life in the 15th century. The fabulous unicorn is caged within the enclosure, with the ladies and musicians. Outside the walls, two men roast an animal caught in the hunt.

Medieval Life.

was high, especially amongst infants.

The castles were cold and humid, for the stone walls could not keep in the heat of the heavy log fires in the grates. There were no carpets or tapestries, just straw strewn on the floor. Furniture consisted of long tables, sleeping cots, stools, benches and one or two armchairs. Dishes and clothes were stored in chests.

Life was also extremely monotonous. There was no culture and no intellectual stimulus, so the lord escaped boredom in the hunt or by going to war with his neighbours.

crowded together but spread throughout the different castle outbuildings: some for the soldiers, others for the servants and separate buildings at last for cattle and domestic animals.

Because the castles were by now serving as centres of administration, culture and trade, the rooms developed specialised uses. The main hall was used for audiences, for the administration of justice and for banquets. There were tapestries and carpets, libraries and schoolrooms where noble children learnt their

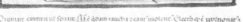

letters. Arrow slits were widened into windows, which at last allowed light into the prevailing penumbra. These windows were glassed, which helped to keep out the cold and humidity.

The kitchen moved from just next to the hall into a separate place, where well seasoned meals were prepared. Dishes of painted and glazed clay came into use alongside the old wooden platters. Kings and princes ate off gold and silver. Only spoons and knives were known at the time as the fork, which originated in Italy, did not come into use until the end of the 15th century. Plates were still a rarity, as people ate from a common dish, so small waterbasins were brought in at the end of the banquet for diners to wash their hands.

Hygiene undoubtedly improved for a while, although this sense of bodily well-being disappeared again during the Renaissance. People bathed in public baths and the high nobility took a private bath on an almost daily basis. When public baths became known as sites of orgies, this might explain why the Renaissance preachers recommended mortification of the flesh and attacked the custom of the public bath.

Small plays, usually of a religious character, were presented by

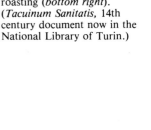

Blois.

troups of wandering players in the hall or at the entrance of the castles. The performances were often accompanied by jugglers, storytellers (later to become troubadours) and dancers. Little-known troubadours might be called on to entertain at a banquet but the famous ones were often leading figures in the cultural and literary circles that were developing. A troubadour was neither a minstrel nor a variety artist but a poet. He usually composed his own music to accompany his verses, using currently recognized techniques that made melody a complement to the rhymed word. They came from all social classes but were often of noble birth, like William IX, Duke of Aquitaine. The first troubadours sang simple love songs in Latin but as the wives of the nobility acquired more independence the troubadour's poetry changed and was written in the vernacular.

Troubadours were at the height of their glory during the 13th century.

Hunting was the principal amusement and sport of the nobility during the Middle Ages. Hunting was on horseback and the prey included deer, boar wolves, and bears. Next to hunting as a preferred pastime was falconry, using falcons, kites and sparrow hawks. Falconry was a highly developed art. The bird had to be taught not only to chase and seize, but not to eat his prey, to return to his master, and not to flinch at people, dogs or horses. Falcons were expensive to buy and to keep, and were greatly coveted. They were housed in special quarters, known as the mews, and ate only the best, such as chicken.

Hunting was considered to be the best training for princes and recommended by the courtly moralists.

BLOIS (France).
François I façade of Blois in the Loire Valley. Built in the 13th century, it was altered and enlarged in the 15th and 16th centuries.

Falcon.

FALCON.
Bird of prey used in falconry, capable of overpowering prey several times larger than itself and characterized by its swift, vertical swoop.

TARASP (Switzerland).
Eleventh century castle which dominates the Inn Valley of the Engadine in Grisons, part of Austria until 1803. Now restored by the Hesse-Darmstadt family who have made it their residence.

Tarasp.

To summarize, castles were at the hub of social development from the 5th to the 14th centuries before they were superseded by civic power and later by the absolute monarchy. While castles were pre-eminent, their owners were often more powerful than the king. Ensconced in his citadel, the local lord was free to give orders, to plot and to set out to subject others.

The Scandinavian grouping includes Norway, Sweden, Finland, Denmark and Iceland. These five countries have similar characteristics and climates, although Denmark, a land of forests and salt marshes joined to Continental Europe by Jutland, seems more like an appendage to the mainland. Endowed with bitter winters and isolated from the rest of Europe, the Scandinavian countries became outstanding marine nations, and developed into a race of great sailors both on their own rivers and at sea. The ancestors of the modern Scandinavians are the Vikings, pioneers, traders and pirates, who reached the British Isles, Iceland, Greenland and the coasts of America and descended as far as the Mediterranean and conquered southern Italy and Sicily, while another branch navigated the Russian rivers and arrived in Constantinople. From the 8th to the 12th centuries, the Vikings were a powerful force in most parts of Europe.

From the 12th century onwards, it was the German influence which left its mark on the Scandinavian countries when they built their great stone castles. Until then, their defences had been of wood, primitive castles set on a hillock and surrounded by a fence. From the 12th century, the castles were of stone or, under Valdemar I (reigned: 1157-1182) in Denmark, stone or brick was added to existing fortifications. The bishops, who were important figureheads of power, were also builders of fortresses. In 1150, Archbishop Eskil erected a castle in Soborg, Seeland, on the site of an octagonal tower. In 1211, Archbishop Absalom began the fortress that later became the nucleus of Copenhagen. By the end of the 12th century the power of the Danish monarchy was such that they owned several castles, such as the great fortress of Hammershus on the island of Bornholm.

Norway was a satellite of Denmark until the end of the 14th century, and the system of rule imposed upon the country gave rise to few feudal institutions or castles. Of those, not many remain.

Sweden, however, had to protect its southern coasts from raids by Danish pirates and built a string of castles. There are about a hundred fortifications in the southern province of Skania, many well restored. The German influence is evident in many. Look, for instance, at the walls of Visby and then at those of Cologne. Nevertheless, the French left their mark on the royal castle of Kalmar, even though this was the exception.

Finnish castles were erected by the Swedes, who controlled the country for centuries. Sited in the south and west, they are usually sturdy, stone structures, now restored and used as museums or cultural centres.

Frederiksborg (Denmark)

SCANDINAVIA

Kronborg.

Denmark

Denmark lies in the shadow of its neighbour to the south, Germany, and has often had to fight against attempts to subordinate it. However, at first it was the Danes who were the predators. Seafaring men who settled in Jutland and the Danish islands in the 6th century, the Danes spread into Skania, in southern Sweden, then turned to sea trading and piracy, entering and conquering part of the British Isles and its coasts on the North Sea.

Denmark was united under Gorm the Old in the 10th century, and the Viking splendour and depredations reached their peak under Knut the Great, who reigned from 1018 to 1035, when the Vikings dominated England and Norway. Although Denmark had to recognize the suzerainty of the Emperor of Germany at the beginning of the 12th century, their glory was renewed under Valdemar I (reigned: 1157-1182) and ended with Valdemar II (reigned: 1202-1241), who conquered Lauenburg, Norway, Pomerolia, Estonia and Courland, but whose conquests were all taken from him in the Battle of Bornhöved in 1227 with the Princes of Northern Germany. From the defeat arose the great commercial alliance of the Hanseatic League.

In 1361, Valdemar IV Atterdag attacked the base of the Hanseatic League at Visby and lost. The ensuing Stralsund Treaty, which granted political and commercial hegemony to the League in the great Baltic zone, provoked the Union of Kalmar, which united the Scandinavian countries as a counterforce to the League, under the rule of Erik of Pomerania. Sweden continued despite this to struggle for independence, which was finally achieved in 1523 under Gustav Eriksson Vasa.

Confronted by Sweden again and again in its attempts to gain control over the northern areas, Denmark was finally forced to surrender its last possessions along the coast of Sweden in the Thirty Years War.

FREDERIKSBORG. Royal Palace built by King Christian IV at the end of the 16th century on three small islands. The palace stands on one island, and the surrounding gardens on the other two. Its baroque salons have been used as a historical museum since 1878 and house important artistic collections.

31

Rosenborg.

KRONBORG. Erik of Pomerania built the original castle on a site in the northernmost part of Sweden, near Helsinger, which guards the strait and from which the garrison could exact tolls on passing ships. The present castle dates from the 16th century and is believed to be the setting used by

Shakespeare in *Hamlet*.

ROSENBORG. Old royal country residence which is now surrounded by modern Copenhagen. Set within gardens, the palace is a museum which houses royal collections and the crown jewels.

Finland

The southern area of modern Finland was colonized by various tribes from Estonia and Latvia in the IIth century BC, when the climatological conditions were good. The Lapps, who were the original settlers, were driven into the north. Later, the Swedes penetrated the south in the 7th century and settled in Karelia on a permanent basis in 1293. Finland was administratively controlled by Sweden from the 12th century but had its own commercial alliance with the Hanseatic League.

TURUNLINNA. Fortress built in 1280 which commands the mouth of the river Aurajoki in Turku. It was badly damaged by bombs in the Second World War but has been restored and is now used as a museum and also for official receptions for foreign visitors.

OLAVLINNA. Built on a small island in Lake Salmaa near the city of Savonlinna in the 15th century. The central courtyard has been adapted for concerts and opera.

Turunlinna.

Olavlinna.

Norway

Much of Norway is within the Arctic Circle. The country is on the western side of the Scandinavian Peninsula, very mountainous, with valleys that run into the sea. The climate on the coasts is determined by the Gulf Stream, whose warm waters keep most of the ports free of ice all year round. This has made the Norwegians great sailors and explorers for land better suited to agriculture than their own mountainous plateaus. The love of adventure and free spirit of the early Norwegians urged them to expand beyond the natural borders of the existing nation,

where they clashed with the first Viking kingships.

Around the year 500, the Danes arrived in Jutland and populated the southern part of Norway which had remained uninhabited because the glaciers had only recently retreated. By the 13th century, the Norwegian Vikings occupied the islands of Shetland, Orkney, the Faroes, the Hebrides and later Iceland.

When King Harald united Norway in 872, some settlers left and went to Iceland, which had been discovered in 860. Greenland

Vardohus.

was discovered in 982 and America (Vinland) around 1000.

Christianity came to Norway at the end of the 9th century, during the rule of King Olaf Tryggvasson and King Knut the Good (Saint). For a short while, Norway fell under the rule of the Danish King Knut the Great, but in 1035 Magnus the Good dethroned the Danish king's son Sven, and was formally crowned.

The Viking momentum had not died down. In 1263, Haakon IV died on the Isle of Man after an expedition against the Hebrides, which were bought by Magnus VI in 1266 from the Scots.

To counteract the power of the maritime cities of the Hanseatic League, the Union of Kalmar was formed in 1397 on the initiative of

the Danes. The Union brought together the five Scandinavian countries under the rule of Erik of Pomerania. From 1397 to 1814, Norway was subject to Denmark.

VARDOHUS. A 13th century castle in the extreme north of Norway, in one of the last areas to be settled. The restoration of the 18th century converted the old castle into a bulwarked citadel in the shape of a star. The buildings now house a historical museum.

STEINVIKSHOLME. Built in 1520 by the Supreme Bishop Olav Engelbrektsson on an island in the Tronheim fjord, it was invaded and destroyed by the Swedes during the Seven Years War.

Steinviksholme.

Sweden

The Swedes, who occupy the eastern part of the Scandinavian Peninsula, which has a rough climate and little farming land, were forced by expanding population to take to their boats to find more land. In the 7th century, Kings of Upsal of the Ynglins Dynasty wrested control of the entire Baltic coast and the Swedes under Rurik settled in the region of Novgorod and established trade links with Constantinople via the navigable Russian rivers.

Christianity came in the 11th century. The Swedish Vikings began their advance through the south of Finland and also took over the area around Lake Mälaren. The period was one of great unrest, from which the principal families to emerge were the Sverkers and the Folkungs. Once the tribes of Svealand (North) and Gotland (South) had united, there was a period of stable rule during which Finland was conquered once and for all under the leadership of Birger Jarl in the mid 13th century.

Central control was fragile. The nobility was not submissive to the throne and there were constant local wars. Any economic initiatives were taken by the cities of the Hanseatic League, which was Germanic in origin or from the cities on the North Sea, and not by the Swedish state. Nonetheless, the Hanseatic League permitted commerce to develop and created lasting ties between Sweden and the outside world. A German Hansa was established in Visby on the island of Gotland in 1161, in direct defiance of Stockholm, which became the capital only in 1250.

German expansionism threatened all the Scandinavian countries. To counteract it, Margaret of Denmark married Hakon VI, the last independent king of Norway. Their son Olaf IV was crowned king of both countries in 1380, to be succeeded by Erik of Pomerania, who was elected king of Sweden as well in 1397. This was the basis of the Union of Kalmar, formalized in the same

Vittskoevle.

year, which created at least temporary unity between the Scandinavian countries and also between the Faroes, Orcades, Hebrides and Greenland islands. Sweden broke loose, unwilling to be controlled by Denmark, but it took a hundred years of unrest and confusion before the country recovered its independence under Gustav Eriksson Vasa.

Sweden and Denmark continued to fight for control of the Baltic until the mid 19th century.

GRIPSHOLM. Gustav Vasa built his stronghold of Gripsholm next to Lake Mälaren on Marlinfred, in 1537. His favourite castle, a stronghold of massive walls and beautiful wall paintings, was altered and added to in the 18th century by another great king, Gustav III.

VITTSKOEVLE. Was built in the 16th century in the southernmost part of the country, on the shores of a lake, and is now a museum.

Gripsholm.

THE BRITISH ISLES

The title of British Isles covers Great Britain and Ireland. The term Great Britain covers the island of England, Wales and Scotland, and also the outlying islands in the Channel, the North Sea and the Atlantic.

Isolated off the north coast of mainland Europe, the British Isles were removed from the main devolpments in the continent. Their history and civilization were able to evolve only with good sea communications. Britain's isolation did not protect her from innumerable invasions before the 11th century, and those invaders became an integral part of the country's indigenous population.

England

England was undoubtedly known to the Phoenicians but it entered history when Julius Caesar crossed the Channel and established an uneasy rule over the south of the country. The Roman border stopped at the Clyde-Forth line with Hadrian's Wall, which left the warring Picts (Scots) cut off to the north of the wall, during the era of the Emperor Hadrian and his Antonine successors.

England was invaded by Jutes, Angles and Saxons in the middle of the 5th century, when the Roman rule had weakened. The Celts, who were the original inhabitants, were driven into Wales, Cornwall, Ireland and Western Scotland. Egbert, king of Wessex, was the first ruler to unite the small Saxon kingdoms. The Viking pillaging began soon after. They sailed up the Thames in 878 and gained control of the surrounding areas. Alfred the Great wrested London from them in 885 and drove them out of southern England for ever, but fresh waves of Danish

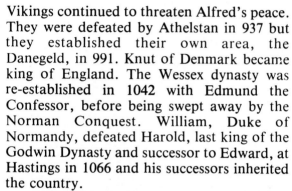

Vikings continued to threaten Alfred's peace. They were defeated by Athelstan in 937 but they established their own area, the Danegeld, in 991. Knut of Denmark became king of England. The Wessex dynasty was re-established in 1042 with Edmund the Confessor, before being swept away by the Norman Conquest. William, Duke of Normandy, defeated Harold, last king of the Godwin Dynasty and successor to Edward, at Hastings in 1066 and his successors inherited the country.

Upon his coronation in 1154, when Henry II Plantagenat was acknowledged by his predecessor Stephen de Blois after the civil war between Stephen and Matilda, Henry II gained not only Stephen's fiefs in France but those of his own wife Eleanor of Aquitaine, through whom the English came to control the western half of France. The first invasion of Ireland took place under Henry II in 1171. England's vast possessions in France caused a state of war between the two countries from 1171 to 1454, when France was lost but for Calais. The tide of conquest shifted to and fro for two and a half centuries. Bouvines was lost in 1214, Crécy won in 1346, and then Agincourt in 1415.

During these years of overseas war, Wales was annexed in 1284 and Scotland invaded in 1296, although Scotland recovered its independence in 1314. The civil unrest between the great power groups of York and Lancaster, called the Wars of the Roses, lasted between 1455 and 1485, before the Tudor dynasty took over in 1485 with Henry VII, and established peace. On the death of Elizabeth I in 1603 without heirs, the Scottish Stuarts took over.

THE TOWER OF LONDON. The Romans first used the site near the mouth of the Thames for fortifications and it was on their ruins that Alfred the Great built. William the Conqueror's castle, which is the one that survives, replaced Alfred's and served as castle, palace and later as state prison. Edward IV's two small sons, known as the Princes in the Tower, were imprisoned and disappeared there. The nine day Queen who preceded Mary Tudor, Lady Jane Grey and her husband, were confined in the Tower before their execution, and later two of Henry VIII's wives, Anne Boleyn and Catherine Howard. So too was the great cleric and opponent to Henry VIII's reforms, Thomas More, all of whom were executed there.

DORSET. The great 12th century square keep of this castle, which is in the southern county of the same name, is still standing.

WINDSOR. The first wooden castle was built by William the Conqueror after his victory over Harold, on a site overlooking the Thames upstream of London. Wood was replaced by stone but the present magnificent castle was the work of Henry II, who used the great round tower as his principal residence. Several other English monarchs have also used Windsor as a home.

MONT ORGUEIL. Located on Jersey, one of the English Channel Islands that is closer to France than to England, Mont Orgueil now overlooks a small fishing port. It is one of several castles built to defend the island against attack from the French. Du Guesclin, the French Constable who threw out the English from large areas of France in the 14th century, tried in vain to capture the castle, but it fell into neglect when Elizabeth's Castle was built in St. Aubin on the same island. The original name was Gorey but it was called Mont Orgueil in memory of its successful defence again and again during the Hundred Years War.

ROCHESTER. Rochester was another of the castles ordered by William the Conqueror, to keep in check Anglo-Saxon resistance after the Battle of Hastings. Overlooking the River Medway, it has a square groundplan and is moated on three sides. It has a large square central tower, three square fortified towers on the corners, and a fourth, round tower on the last corner,

Dorset.

Windsor.

Mont Orgueil.

which replaces the square one destroyed in 1216 when the castle was attacked by King John. Rochester was an important castle as it was located on the strategic London-Dover road.

WARWICK. William the Conqueror first chose the site on the Avon River for a castle but the present one dates from the 14th century. It has an entrance protected by a barbican and two massive towers, the round Caesar's Tower and the octagonal William's Tower.

BODIAM. A 14th century castle built by Sir Edward Dailyngrigg in 1385 on his return from fighting in France. A bridge protected by two square towers spans a moat filled with water, and the high outside walls are guarded by round towers at the corners.

Rochester.

43

WARWICK

Bodiam.

Scotland

Saint Andrews.

The Picts and Caledonians were defeated by the Roman general Agricola in AD 80 and were cut off from England by the emperor Hadrian with his Hadrian's Wall, which was built in 138. In the 5th century, the Scots from Ireland settled in Scotland and mixed with the Picts. From the 8th century onwards, Scotland's coasts were harassed by the Vikings, like those of England and the rest of Europe, but finally the Danes settled in the west of the country.

Malcolm II took control of Scotland in 1018 (the immediate predecessor of Duncan and Macbeth). King William the Lion declared himself vassal to the English Henry II in 1174 but the country remained independent until 1296, when the royal line became extinct and England's Edward I,

Sinclair,

Hammer of the Scots, was named ruler of Scotland. The Battle of Bannockburn restored autonomy to the country in 1214 under Robert the Bruce, whose successor Robert II founded the Stuart dynasty that would finally unite both countries in 1603 under James I.

SAINT ANDREWS. The walls of this ruined 13th century castle on the east coast of Scotland practically reach the seashore.

SINCLAIR. Sinclair castle and Girnigoe castle, both dating from the 17th century, were built alongside at the extreme end of Noss Head, in Caithness. Only ruins survive.

EILEAN DONAN. This solid structure of the 13th century was built by Alexander II in 1220 to protect Loch Duich from pirate raids. It was destroyed by the English in 1717 when it was held by a Spanish garrison in the name of the last Stuart, who never reigned.

Eilean Donan.

Wales

In the beginning of the 6th century, King Arthur unified the Celtic populations against the Anglo-Saxon invaders. In 1284, Edward I of England annexed the country and gave the title of Prince of Wales to the heir to the throne. Unable to penetrate the Welsh mountains in Snowdonia, Edward surrounded the region with powerful fortresses. The most famous rebel against the English was Owen Glendower, whose abortive rebellion lasted from 1400 to 1415.

The first castles were built to guard the

coast after the Norman conquest of England. They were of stone and their ruins still stand. The great age of the castles was in the late 13th and early 14th centuries, under King Edward I.

CAREW. Built before 1095, the castle passed into the hands of the Normans with the marriage of Gerald of Windsor to the sister of Rhys, the prince of southern Wales. It was modified and expanded in the 12th and 13th centuries. The four large towers are recent. The last time it was used for a military purpose was when it was besieged in 1642 by Cromwell, that great destroyer of castles, during the Civil War.

Carew,

Oystermouth.

OYSTERMOUTH. Probably dates from the early 12th century when the Normans controlled southern Wales. The castle was destroyed by the Welsh in 1287 after a violent insurrection but was reconstructed later with Gothic windows.

CAERPHILLY. One of the largest castles of Wales and the first in Great Britain to adopt a concentric groundplan. The fortress defends land and sea. Seven successive gates guard the main entrance, which has its own barbican, and lead into three separate enclosures. Construction was begun by Gilbert of Clare, Count of Gloucester, in 1268, during the English struggle against Llewellyn, Prince of Wales. The site had previously been used by the Romans and later by the Normans in 1090.

HARLECH. This is one of Edward I's castles, built between 1283 and 1290. The groundplan is quadrangular. There are large, round towers at three of the corners, while

Caerphilly.

Harlech.

the fourth is defended by the keep, reinforced by two round towers.

CONWAY. Built on the Conway river close to Caernarvon Castle, both castles are masterpieces of English architecture of the 13th century. Both were ordered by King Edward I after the conquest of Wales and the death of Llewellyn, Prince of Wales, who had been captured with his brother Dafydd in the second campaign led by Edward. Conway castle has solid, high walls flanked by several large, round towers which were refashioned soon after and then converted for artillery use by the Stuarts in the 17th century.

CARDIFF. Cardiff castle is probably built on the site where the small castle of the

Morganway princes stood in 1081. The site certainly had a military structure in Roman times. The present castle was built by Robert Fitzhamon in the 12th century, and was massively damaged by Owen Glendower during his uprising against King Henry IV in 1404. It was held by the Royalists during the Civil War in the 17th century until the defeat of St. Fagan nearby. The castle is on a small hill, fortified by high walls, with access via a large, octagonal tower.

Conway.

Cardiff.

Tipperary.

Ireland

The history of the Irish has been closely allied to that of the English for over 700 years. For much of that time, the Irish have rebelled and the English have invaded and settled. A second influence on Irish history has been its status as a small, poor island from which there have been waves of emigration.

The Celts settled the island in the 5th century BC and created a unique culture which was untouched by Rome, for the Romans never attempted action against Ireland when they were in England. The various Celtic tribes united and formed five great kingdoms.

Ireland's golden age began in 432, when Saint Patrick brought Christianity to the island and, they say, drove out the snakes. Irish Celtic monks settled Iona and began evangelization of some areas before the Romans, and from Ireland came an understanding of holiness and learning which was exported to Europe in the 7th and 8th centuries. The Celtic Church lost its position as Europe's guide and teacher in 663, when the Synod of Whitby gave supremacy to the Church of Rome.

At the end of the 8th century, the Viking invasions began and destroyed the monasteries. Although the Vikings were driven back, they had settled in some areas by 841, forming cities which would later be important, such as Dublin.

In 1014, Brian Boru had an important victory in Contarf against the Vikings, who

were gradually assimilated into the population and contributed to the commercial development of the country. Internal conflicts between Ireland's petty kings became so destructive that the King of Leinster called in the Anglo-Normans to bring order. In one way or another, they never left. They first landed in 1170, took over Dublin and fortified the surroundings. Henry II of England, treating Ireland like a subject colony, stripped the Gaelic landowners of their land and distributed it between the Crown possessions and to his nobles.

The Irish have rebelled against the English at various times in their history. Although the English controlled only Dublin and its immediate surroundings in the 15th century, their actions were often to crush and subjugate the population as a whole. The Anglo-Normans scattered large and mighty castles throughout the island and many still stand, arrogant and well preserved.

TIPPERARY. The Castle of Tipperary stands on a promontory overlooking the sea. The landward approach is guarded by a large moat. It was a centre of agitation against English rule.

BUNRATTY. Bunratty Castle, built in the 15th century on the banks of Bunratty river, was a fief of the O'Brien family until the middle of the 16th century. It has been considerably restored and now mock medieval banquets are held there. A medieval town has been reconstructed behind the castle as a «living museum», where artisans and craftsmen can be seen at work.

Bunratty,

BÜRRESHEIM

CENTRAL EUROPE

entral Europe includes Poland, Germany, Switzerland, Liechtenstein, Austria, Czechoslovakia and Hungary —the countries situated between the great Russian plain and the Rhine, and bordered to the south by the Alps and the Carpathians. The area covers about 400,000 square miles.

Historically and culturally, Central Europe has been formed by Germanic influences, fostered by the long years during which the Holy Roman Empire, successor to Charlemagne's empire, held the area.

Nevertheless, when the Carolingian empire broke and Germany's imperial power proved to be unable to hold back the invasions of the Normans, Slavs and Hungarians, various national entities began to form under the turmoil. The first Germanic emperors, especially the three Ottos, concentrated on their eastern frontiers but despite several victories, such as Otto I's over the Hungarians in 955 at Lechfeld, the territories to the east of the Elba river had to be abandoned, leaving Poland, Bohemia and Hungary to their separate destinies.

Agriculture and trade flourished. The cities and especially the sea ports prospered and the Holy Roman Empire began to fill with castles belonging to lords and princes of the church.

At the same time as the Empire changed and settled, the knights of the Teutonic Order in the east, bearers of the Crusader spirit, carried German expansion towards Pomerania, Prussia and Poland.

When Christianity came to the Slavs under Otto I, new bishoprics and large abbeys were created. Bishops and abbots were vested with temporal power and played a powerful role in government.

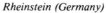

Rheinstein (Germany)

When the leadership of the Empire passed to Austria in the 17th century, the 300 or so independent territories, loosely under its rule, lost their base.

Werfen.

Austria

Austria has been at Europe's crossroads throughout history, the point at which most invasions from the East were defeated, and where the Turkish advances were checked at Vienna. The Romans occupied the area in 15 BC and staked out the border with frontier posts. At the end of the 9th century, Charlemagne incorporated it in his empire under the name East Marche, and defeated the Avarians and Bavarians. The Babenberg dynasty controlled and unified the country from the end of the 9th century until 1265, adding Styria in 1192. Then the Habsburgs

took over and ruled from 1272 until the end of the 19th century. They broke every Turkish invasion and successfully defended Vienna from the Turks in 1529 and again in 1683, when the Austrian defence had the help of the Polish king John Sobiesky.

On the crossroads of so many invasions, Austria is dotted with castles, many in ruins, but others now acting as museums.

WERFEN. Set on a peak of rock, Werfen castle overlooks the valley of Salzach and guards Salzburg.

Anif.

Schonbühel.

Festung.

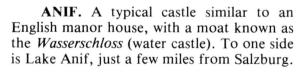
Hochosterwitz.

ANIF. A typical castle similar to an English manor house, with a moat known as the *Wasserschloss* (water castle). To one side is Lake Anif, just a few miles from Salzburg.

HOCHOSTERWITZ. A powerful fortress against the Turks. It has seven fortified enclosures, surrounded by three large moats and crossed by 14 doors across the access ramp of the castle. Between 1570 and 1586, the castle was converted by George Khevenhüller, governor of Carinthia, into a stronghold for fleeing Protestants.

SCHONBÜHEL. Built on the shores of the Danube. The present 19th century castle stands on the site of a medieval fortress.

FESTUNG. Situated on a magnificent hill close to Salzburg and surrounded by small churches.

Czechoslovakia

Modern Czechoslovakia was created in 1918 from Bohemia-Moravia, Silesia, and the Slovak territory which was previously part of Hungary.

Bohemia was first occupied by the Celtic tribe known as the Boios (giving their name to the country, Boiohemun) but it was the Slavic tribes which arrived during the 5th and 6th centuries that formed its population. The Slavs founded the first independent state of Europe, the Samo Empire, and defeated the Franks of King Dagelbert.

Great Moravia was created in the 9th century, and included within its boundaries Bohemia-Moravia, part of Poland, Hungary and Silesia. Great Moravia reached its peak under Sviatopluk but was broken by the Magyar invasions at the beginning of the 10th century. Slovakia remained under the Hungarians for the next nine centuries.

The new Czech state was formed under the Premslyed dynasty which created its capital in Prague. The dynasty lasted until 1306, when King Wenceslas II was

assassinated and the crown passed to the House of Luxembourg. During the time of the Premslyeds, mining, agriculture and trade all developed and the burgeoning new cities attracted large numbers of German immigrants. Under the rule of Luxembourg, Bohemia-Moravia reached its greatest glory, especially under King Charles IV.

Jan Hus (1373-1415), the Bohemian reformer who preached against the secular power of the church and who attacked the aspects of feudalism which had become antiquated, was burnt at the stake. The Polish house of Jagellon succeeded the Luxembourgs and ruled until 1525 when power passed to the Habsburgs, who had been called in by the Czechs to defend them against the Turks.

In 1618, the Nationalist Hussites threw the Catholic rulers out of the window of Prage Castle, and the event caused the Thirty Years War.

There are major geographical changes between the valleys, plateaus and hills of

Karlstein.

Bohemia-Moravia, and the mountains of Slovakia. Three thousand castles cover the country, nowadays in ruins or converted into museums, rest homes or holiday colonies.

KARLSTEIN. The castle was built in 1348, at the order of Charles IV, Emperor of Germany and King of Bohemia, and served as repository for the crown jewels. Several of the rooms have the wall paintings and stuccoes one would expect in an imperial building.

ORAVSKY HRAD. The first castle was erected in 1263, built of wood on stone foundations. The old fortress was taken over by Ctibor de Ctiborice and was restored and enlarged in 1474 by Matthew Aorvino, who filled it with palatial halls within the defensive walls. The building was extensively modified again in the 16th and 17th centuries.

Oravsky Hrad.

Germany

The Germany that is divided into two states at present has been a leading power of Europe. Germany's history has been stamped by the repeated pattern of invasion from the East, struggle, periods of power and victory, and repeated colonization of the invaders, repulsion, fresh power.

This Arian race of Christians became allies of the Holy Roman Empire to which they annexed the regions they had settled in. The western areas of the future Germany were settled by Franks and Alemanni, while Saxons, Frisians and Bavarians moved into the eastern part. The Germanic tribes were conquered and forced into unity by Charlemagne, who laid the foundations of both modern France and Germany.

Charlemagne's empire was dismantled in 843 under the Treaty of Verdun, a vacuum into which Otto I the Great stepped, when he

founded the Holy Roman Empire in 936, that was to last at least as a legal entity until 1806. This great emperor began Germany's expansions to the east and the north. Yet the conflict between the Papacy and the Holy Roman Empire on the question of the Investitures, which began in 1075, was to mark the entire Middle Ages and lead to a succession of conflicts on German and Italian soil. The struggle endured throughout the reign of the Hohenstauffen dynasty, which lasted from 1125 to 1254, and covered the rule of both Frederick I Barbarossa and Frederick II.

The Golden Bull of Rimini in 1226 legalized the activities of the Order of Teutonic Knights in pagan Prussia and gave them authority to conquer and colonize the area.

Anholt.

Ahrensburg.

The terrible dispute between the spiritual rulers of Rome and the temporal ones of the Holy Roman Empire began with Pope Gregory VII and Emperor Henry IV. Gregory VII ruled that the head of the Church was absolute and supreme. The Pope, therefore, had the power to nominate and dismiss not only bishops but those who ruled by divine right alone, the kings. Kings, ordained Pope Gregory VII, were subject to the Church. Frederick I went in the face of the papal ordinance and attempted to apply absolutist rule in northern Italy, which brought the Papacy into conflict with him, along with the communes and free cities, especially the free city of Milan. Peace was signed at Lake Constance in 1181 but the struggle was too bitter for it to hold. When Frederick II was crowned king of Sicily by right of inheritance and not by election of the Pope, and then attempted to bring the

dominions under his control into closer unity, the threat to the Papacy was blatant, and the papal armies defeated the Emperor definitively at Cremona in 1248.

Albert II of Austria brought the Hapsburg dynasty to Germany, Hungary and Bohemia in 1438. In 1488, the decline of the Empire began, when the Swabian League, composed of princes, lords and common people came together to defy the imperial power.

The Thirty Years War, fought out mainly on German soil, ravaged the country from 1618 to 1648 and the Peace of Westphalia left Germany divided into 350 principalities.

These have been the constants in German history: first, the fight against the nations of the east, initially to contain them and later to colonize and rule, under the impetus of the Teutonic Knights; secondly,

SIGMARINGEN

Burg Katz.

the struggle against the Papacy and lure of the Italian territories. The Lombard cities and their rule of banker-merchants, served as a distant model for the great German maritime cities and the rise of the Hanseatic League.

Germany became divided into innumerable countries, big and small, noble and ecclesiastical, at the mercy of weak emperors and strong feudal princes, and dominated by the power of the feudal castles. Many of these castles have been destroyed in one or the other of the two great 20th century wars.

BÜRRESHEIM. The northern section and the round tower date from the 14th century, while the southern section is 17th century. The garden is in French style.

RHEINSTEIN. Located on a steep cliff overlooking the Rhine, the castle was rebuilt in the 19th century. In origin, it is one of the oldest of the Rhine castles.

ANHOLT. A 15th century castle surrounded by moats and now restored as a hotel.

AHRENSBURG. Built in the 17th century, the castle has been restored and converted into a museum of 18th century housing.

SIGMARINGEN. The high, rocky site overlooking the Danube was first guarded by a feudal fortress. A new castle was built in the Renaissance, in what was the capital of the Hohenzollern Principality.

BURG KATZ (Cats Castle). One of the many castles that controlled traffic on the Rhine. It was built in the 14th century on the foundations of a previous fortress, and was later restored.

NEUSCHWANSTEIN. A 19th century edifice built in a neo-feudal romantic style by Louis II of Bavaria, it gives the impression of being designed by a decorator rather than an architect. Many of the rooms echo episodes of the Wagnerian operas.

Gutenberg.

Schlossberg.

Schlossberg.

Liechtenstein

The tiny principality, located between Austria and Switzerland, covers only 62 square miles and has 25,000 inhabitants. It is 5 miles wide at some points and can easily be crossed by foot. The northern part (Vuterland) is flat while it gets progressively more mountainous towards the south (Oberland).

The present principality was formed in 1434 when the country of Vaduz was united with Schelenberg. The resulting union was under the rule of the Austrian prince Hans Adam in the 18th century, and in 1719 Emperor Charles VI of Austria converted the territories into a principality within the Holy Roman Empire. Liechtenstein remained a part of Austria until the First World War but when it broke away in 1919, it established ties with Switzerland, joined the Swiss Customs Union in 1924 and allowed itself to be represented diplomatically by that country.

The two great fortresses are Schlossberg and Gutenberg.

GUTENBERG. Built on a promontory by the Rhine and near the village of Balzsers, the castle of the Counts of Fauenberg was built in the 13th century next to an earlier chapel dedicated to Saint Donatus. From 1314 to the 19th century, the ruling Hapsburgs used Gutenberg as one of their centres of power.

SCHLOSSBERG. Built on a hill overlooking the small capital city of Vaduz, Schlossberg fortress is now the home of the ruling Prince and Princess.

Wawel.

Poland

Poland belongs to the great Central European plain. It has been repeatedly invaded and threatened with extinction and has been partitioned between powerful neighbours more than once. Poland's vulnerability is principally caused by the lack of natural borders such as mountains or rivers, for even in the mountainous southern area, heights rarely exceed 3,000 ft.

Mieszko I united the Polish tribes and founded the independent state in 963 (Polans: inhabitants of the plains). He married a Christian in 966 and after his conversion, introduced Christianity as the state religion. A considerable warrior, Mieszko I confronted the East Germans, and conquered

Silesia.

Poland became the leader of the other western Slav countries under Boleslaw I, the Brave (reigned: 992 to 1025), who subdued the Vislan tribes and made his capital at Cracow. For the next two centuries, Poland was under the Holy Roman Empire and during the constant wars, lost, recovered and lost again Pomerania and Lusacia. The invasion of the Mongols was halted in 1241. In 1306 Duke Wladislaw re-established unity and was crowned king.

Casimir II, the Great (reigned: 1333 to 1370) yielded, despite his soubriquet, Silesia to Bohemia and Prussia to the Teutonic Knights. He nevertheless greatly strengthened the country, welcoming German immigration and building new cities. In 1410, Wladislaw II

Pieskova.

Jagellon made an alliance with Lithuania and beat the Teutonic Order at Tennenberg and again in 1422 at Lake Melno. In 1457, the Poles assaulted and took Marunburg, capital of the Teutonic Order, and in 1466 the Treaty of Thorn restored to Poland Pomerania, Ermeland and Kulm. The end of the 15th century was Poland's time of greatest glory. The country extended from the Baltic to the Black Sea. In 1485, Moldavia recognized Polish sovereignty. Yet Poland remained surrounded by the powers of Russia, the Ottomans and the Hapsburgs.

Warsaw became the capital in 1595. Starting in 1621, Poland began to lose. Livonia went in 1621, and some of the Baltic ports were ceded to Sweden. During invasions by the Cossacks, Swedes, Germans,

Russians and Turks, Smolensk and Ukraine were lost, although John Sobieski won a great victory against the Turks at Vienna in 1683.

Poland was partitioned in 1772, 1793 and 1795 between Austria, Prussia and Russia, and finally disappeared as an independent nation until 1918.

WAWEL. Old royal palace in the centre of the city, near the Vistula river. The Pantheon of Great Poles is housed in the Cathedral, which is attached to the palace.

PIESKOWA. Built in the 16th century, Pieskowa is one of the 125 castles between Cracow and Czestochowa.

Switzerland

Placed virtually at the political centre of Europe, Switzerland is also its most mountainous country. It has been inhabited since primitive times but entered history in 58 BC, when the territory of the Helveti was conquered by Caesar. Invaded by the Burgundians and the Alemanni in the 5th century, Switzerland was first absorbed into the Frank empire and by the 9th century into that of Germany. As the Holy Roman Empire weakened, the country split into small, independent fiefs, while power fell into the hands of the feudal houses like the Zähringen, Savoy, Kyburg and Hapsburg. The Emperor granted independence to the cities of Zurich and Berne, while the inhabitants, isolated in their mountains, grew accustomed to managing their affairs with considerable autonomy.

CHILLON. The fortress on Lake Leman is 9th century in origin, built by the Bishops of Sion to guard the route to Italy through the Saint Bernard Pass. It was progressively enlarged by the Counts of Savoy after they took over the castle in 1150 until by the mid 13th century, it had acquired its final form.

OBERHOFEN. Built on Lake Thun, Oberhofen is based on a 12th century castle which was considerably restored and altered in the 17th and 19th centuries. It is now a branch of the Historical Museum of Berne and houses important collections of popular art from the Berne region.

Chillon.

Oberhofen.

enelux is the grouping of Belgium, Holland and Luxembourg. Forced by their geography to be places of passage for their powerful neighbours, they have been a constant prey to invasion, especially by France. The Benelux grouping was united under the House of Burgundy in the middle of the 15th century and later handed to Spain. The Protestant Reformation of the 16th century stirred a spirit of rebellion and desires for independence which led to freedom for Holland, while the southern states of Belgium and Luxembourg remained Spanish until the 18th century.

The three countries have formed one of the most important commercial and maritime centres of Europe contributing as much as Italy did in the south, to the rebirth of commerce at the beginning of the 13th century.

Durstede, on the Rhine and next to present-day Utrecht, was a great commercial centre at the end of the 8th century but was destroyed by the Normans towards the middle of the 9th century. The Frisian trading fleets came down the Rhine, the Scheldt and the Mense and returned with Rhenish wine and textiles, and the fleets sometimes sailed on to the Baltic countries. By the late 12th century, the Flemish cities had become flourishing and important centres. Filled with textile workers who poured in from the country, Ghent, Bruges and Ypres grew and prospered.

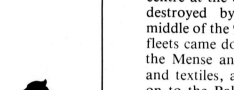

Horst.

Belgium

Belgium has been settled by, conquered and controlled by Saxons, Romans, Franks (the present Flemish), Vikings and Central Europeans, who have all left their mark on this fertile land. Civilization, communications and trade flowed along the great, navigable rivers which cross the country, the Meuse and the Scheldt. Squeezed between France and Germany, Belgium has been a battleground more than once in the clash between the two greater powers.

The disintegration of the Carolingian empire created a host of small fiefs and the seeds of prosperous cities in Belgium which, little by little, acquired privileges that converted them into small, independent republics well able to take advantage of the quarrels between kings and princes.

The period of glory for this merchant class lasted from the 12th to the 15th centuries. At the time the area was under the control of the Dukes of Burgundy, a prosperity based on textiles prevailed. The country passed to Spain in the 16th century, and then to Austria and was not free until 1831.

The shores of the Belgian rivers are dotted with castles and ruins of castles, most dating from the 11th and 12th centuries. The Castle of the Counts of Flanders was built in Ghent at the end of the 12th century, to a design inspired by the Crusader fortresses of Syria. It was completely rebuilt in the 19th century and houses a museum of torture.

BEERSEL. Another museum of torture. Reproductions of instruments are on view in one of the three, large round towers. The castle was built at the beginning of the 14th century in brick and restored at the end of the 17th century.

HORST. This castle, surrounded by a moat and preserving the original 14th century keep, stands in the middle of lush forest. It is built of stone and brick.

LAARNE. Built as a centre of defence in the area of Ghent, the castle has a basic 12th century core with 17th century modifications. The moat has not been filled in. Inside are tapestries and collections of silver.

Laarne.

De Haar.

Holland

The country is correctly known as The Netherlands as Holland is, in fact, the name of one of the regions which has come to supplant the official one. Holland's history has been shaped by its three great rivers, the Rhine, the Mense and the Scheldt, which flow between the countless islands that make up its coast. A quarter of the country is below sea level but the land is protected by the natural dunes formed by the masses of alluvial mud swept in and deposited by the rivers, as well as by a series of artificial ones. The rivers have been the means of communication and trade.

Various peoples settled the country during the era of the great invasions and existed alongside of each other —Frisians, Bavarians Franks, and other Romanized tribes, until the dismantling of the Carolingian

Holland then became part of the Holy Roman Empire but the territorial unity dissolved into small, independent fiefs and

cities which wished for independence.

While the Vikings commanded the seaways, other countries which were to become maritime powers were unable to develop, but once the Vikings had retreated, the ports, of Frisia and Holland expanded in the 9th and 10th centuries. In 1428, the Duke of Burgundy, Philip the Good, became lord of The Netherlands, which passed to the Spanish in 1515. Charles I of Spain persecuted the Dutch Lutherans and Baptists, provoking rebellion which lasted sporadically between 1568 and 1648. The country was finally given its independence in 1648, through the Treaty of The Hague.

DE HAAR. The history of the castle of De Haar goes back a long way. The earliest written reference is in 1163. It was rebuilt by the architect P.J.H. Cuypers in 1892 to the original plan and using part of the old wall, but diverting from the medieval design in the interior. Located in the small town of Haar Zuilens, within the municipality of Vleuten, the castle has belonged to the Van Zuilen family since 1440.

Luxembourg

The Grand Duchy of Luxembourg is the largest of Europe's small states. It covers about 1,000 square miles and has a population of 350,000. Its history began in the 10th century, when Sigfried of Bigdau made it into a state. Upon the election of Henry of Luxembourg as Emperor of Germany in 1308, this tiny state's amazing period of glory began. It was to provide four emperors, four kings of Bohemia and one king of Hungary. The Emperor Charles IV of Luxembourg gave his country the status of Duchy in 1354. It was occupied first by Burgundy and then by Spain, losing its independence in the 15th century, which was not recovered until 1815. Luxembourg was always coveted as it has an excellent strategic location. Its impregnable capital has been nicknamed the Gibraltar of the North.

There are about 130 castles and fortresses in Luxembourg, some in ruins but others in a good state of repair.

WILTZ. Built in the 13th century and restored on several occasions, today it has a remodelled courtyard where theatrical and musical performances take place.

VIANDEN. The magnificent façade is only a silhouette, as the 11th century castle, restored in the 13th century, is now in ruins. The castle chapel dates from the time of Charlemagne and within the walls there is a strange room in the Byzantine style, where the 13th century windows are still intact.

Wiltz.

Vianden.

SAUMUR

FRANCE
and MONACO

France is the cradle of feudalism. It was there that feudalism was shaped when the Carolingian empire fell, and feudal life is what gave the principal characteristics to castles and shaped their development.

The Celts came from the Danube region and advanced slowly towards France, then Spain, the British Isles and Italy and in 387 BC, they defeated the Roman troops. They settled in all the countries they had overrun but concentrated their settlements in Gaul, modern France.

The Romans had occupied and romanized the Mediterranean coast of Gaul bit by bit but it was Caesar who conquered all Gaul between 58 and 51 BC, in a series of victories against the Helveti (58 BC), the Belgii (57 BC), in Brittany and Aquitaine (56 BC), pursuing the Germans and crossing the Rhine. He later invaded England (55 BC). The Gaul leader Vercingetorix was defeated in 52 BC.

Gaul was invaded by Burgundians, Visigoths and Franks in the 4th and 5th centuries but it was the Franks who survived the other tribes and stayed to found the ruling dynasty of the Merovingians and later the Carolingians. In 732, Charles Martel halted the Moslem advances at Poitiers.

Between 768 and 814, Charlemagne founded his great empire round the nucleus of France, an empire which covered Germany, Austria, Friesland, Saxony, Bavaria, Italy, the frontier Marches of Spain, Brittany, and Carinthia. His successors were unable to hold together such far-flung possessions, which anyway Charlemagne had decreed should be divided into three kingdoms on his death.

In 896 the Vikings settled at the mouth of the Seine and in 911 the French king Charles the Simple ceded Normandy to their chief Rollo. William of Normandy used this

Pau.

as a base in 1066, when he invaded England, defeated the Saxon Harold and became king himself.

In 1152, Eleanor of Aquitaine, divorced wife of Louis VII of France, married the Count of Anjou, who became Henry II of England in 1154. Her dowry was half of France. For the next three hundred years, French and English would be at war over these territories. In 1214, Philip II Augustus of France defeated the English ally Emperor Otto IV of Germany. Louis IX (Saint Louis) crushed a rebellion of nobles backed by England. England was forced to give up all her French territories but for Aquitaine by the Treaty of Paris (1259), yet Edward II of England set out on what was to be the Hundred Years War in 1339, starting with a series of military victories. He was checked only by lack of money, after the victory of Crécy.

The military genius of Bertran Du Guesclin began the reconquest of the lost territories under Charles V of France before the balance of power swayed to the English again when Henry V of England landed in 1415 and won the battle of Agincourt.

When Charles VII (reigned: 1422 to 1461) was crowned King of France, the country was divided into three large areas: the English area covered Normandy, Poitou and Aquitaine; Burgundy was an independent state; leaving the French crown with Anjou and the south of France. Joan of Arc left her fields to restore the confidence of the people and turn the tide in favour of her country. Normandy was taken in 1450 and Aquitaine in 1461.

During the reign of Louis XI (reigned: 1461 to 1483), Burgundy was annexed after the death of its ruler Charles the Bold, and Maine and Provence fell to the French on the death of King René. France lost Flanders in 1482 as it formed part of the dowry of Marie of Burgundy when she married Maximillian of Austria.

When the Burgundian inheritance was divided by the Treaty of Senlis in 1493, the groundwork was laid for the future rivalry between France and the Hapsburgs.

François I added the Duchies of Brittany, Bourbon and Auvergne to the kingdom and tried to expand into the north of Italy. His failure to become elected Emperor of Germany caused the first French-Spanish confrontation. He was defeated and imprisoned by the Emperor Charles at Pavia in 1526. The second Franco-Spanish confrontation developed in 1526 and 1529. François I made an alliance with the Turkish pirate Khaireddin Barbarossa, confronting Spain in 1536 and again in 1542. His heir, Henri II was severely defeated by Spain at San Quintin and at Gravelinas. The Treaty of Château-Cambrésis was signed between France and Spain in 1559, which yielded Naples and Burgundy to the Spanish.

In 1562, the French Catholics attacked the French Protestants (the Huguenots), the start of the bitter Wars of Religion. On the night of Saint Bartholomew, 20,000 Hugue-

Commequiers.

Roquetaillade.

nots were massacred. The Edict of Nantes of 1598 finally granted the Huguenots freedom of worship.

The era of France's greatness was during the reigns of Louis XIII and Louis XIV.

Together with Spain, France has perhaps the largest number of castles in Europe, for both countries had strong feudal systems, under which every lord and almost every vassal tried to own a castle. Many of the fortresses were converted into splendid palaces during the Renaissance, and the most lovely of all are the Châteaux of the Loire.

SAUMUR. The first castle was built in the 10th century by Theobold, Count of Blois, during his war against the Count of Anjou. The present castle was built in 1367 by Louis I of Anjou and was modernized by the Italian architect Bartholomew at the end

of the 16th century. It stands on a small hill at the confluence of the Loire and Thouet rivers. The square enclosure is flanked by four towers built with rounded base and octagonal slopes and reinforced by buttresses. The castle is surrounded by a rampart walk, where the battlements are still intact.

PAU. A much restored and mutilated castle. Pau was built in the middle of the 12th century, altered in the 13th, and again in the 14th century by Sicart of Lordat for Gaston Phoebus. The castle was badly restored in the 19th century. Legend has it that the first Viscount of Bearn marked the site of the castle he intended to build with three poles. The site was a small hill overlooking the river Give. And hence the name: Pau, or poles.

Carcassonne.

Collioure.

Chambord.

COMMEQUIERS. The ruined 15th century castle was built on the remains of an earlier, 13th century one. The later castle was dismantled in the 17th century, but the remains of the defence curtain, that had eight towers and an octagonal keep, were allowed to stand.

ROQUETAILLADE. The great keep is 15th century, strongly protected by a curtain of circular towers at the corners. The castle was rebuilt in 1306 by Cardinal Gaillard de la Mote, nephew of Pope Clement V.

SULLY-SUR-LOIRE. Built at the end of the 14th century by the Tremouille family, the castle was restored by Maximillian de Bethume. The groundplan is rectangular, flanked by large towers on the corners and protected on three sides by the Loire. The gate is defended by its own small castle and drawbridge. The battlements, machicolation galleries and rampart walk still stand.

CARCASSONNE. Carcassonne's walled city is guarded to the northeast by a massive quadrangular castle built into the wall. The enclosure walls are 6 to 8 ft thick, but there is no keep. The original castle was built in the

12th century and rebuilt in the 13th, when it became a royal holding and representative of the royal power in the region. It was besieged by Simon de Montfort in 1209 and fell to him when food and water ran out. In 1240, Louis IX (Saint Louis) punished the population for insurrection and evicted them from their homes to the other bank of the Aude river.

COLLIOURE. The first owners of Collioure were the Kings of Aragon, but it passed to the Kings of Majorca in 1272. When the castle reverted to Spain, the Catalan-Aragonese monarchy added to the fortifications in 1280 and again in 1344. Finally, conquered by the French, the fortress was given a bulwark in the 17th and 18th centuries. It has two great rectangular towers, one guarding the northeast gate.

CHAMBORD. The first castle was built by the Counts of Blois not far from their capital. It was destroyed by François I so that he could use the site for a royal palace. The plan is typically medieval despite the period. There is a large fortified tower in the centre, surrounded by four angular towers and a great defence curtain. Yet, despite the medieval groundplan, the palace does not give a

Foix.

military feel but conforms to its purpose as a royal mansion.

FOIX. On a rocky dominant site over the city below, Foix dates from the 11th century. The large 12th century tower on the north is linked to a 14th century quadrangular tower by two walls, which enclose several outbuildings. The complex is surrounded by a

rampart and the entrance is protected by a circular 15th century tower. The Count of Foix, to whom the castle belonged, rose against Philip the Bold in 1272 and was besieged within his castle. The castle fell when the king, unable to take it by assault, ordered his soldiers to chip away at the rock base on which the castle was built.

Monaco

Flanked by France and Italy, Monaco is one of the smallest independent states still surviving in Europe, though it is typical of the Italian city states which existed in the Middle Ages. In fact, Monaco has been a fief of the Grimaldi family in uninterrupted succession since the 13th century, when Francesco Grimaldi, a Genoan of the Guelf faction, was expelled from his country. He disguised his soldiers as monks and took

control of Monaco, and ever since then, the Grimaldi coat of arms has sported two armed monks.

The state has survived through the centuries under the protection of powerful neighbours, sometimes France, sometimes Savoy or Sardinia.

GRIMALDI. Located on a hill overlooking the sea, the old fortress is now the residence of the ruling Prince and Princess.

Grimaldi.

THE IBERIAN PENINSULA

he Iberian Peninsula is at the extreme western end of Europe, separated from France by the Pyrenees mountain range. Despite the mountain frontiers to the north and the seas on its other borders, the Peninsula has been invaded at different periods in its history both from Europe and from Africa.

The first invasions in historical times were Roman, followed by the incursions by barbarian tribes in the 4th and 5th centuries which afflicted all of Europe. In 711, the continent, which still formed a single country, was invaded and settled by the Moors and Berbers of North Africa. The ensuing struggle between Islam and Christianity lasted for nearly 700 years.

Although the presence of Arabs within a Christian population was to lead to ceaseless struggles, the influence was also positive, as the Spanish Moors had an advanced civilization. Ideas and knowledge were assimilated by pilgrims going to Santiago to visit the Tomb of the Apostle in Galicia, and were taken back to the still primitive medieval European countries. Portugal split away in the 12th century to form a separate entity. After the Moors had been thrown out and Christianity established as the one ruling religion over the whole area, both countries embarked on the great seafaring discoveries which led Europe to discover the New World.

The struggle against the Moors, border disputes and attempts to annex Portugal to Spain were to occupy a large part of the history of both countries.

In 1383, Juan I of Castille attempted to exercise his right to the Portugese crown but was defeated in 1385 at Aljubarrota. Only in 1580 did Portugal become part of the Spanish empire, when Philip II invaded upon the death of the Portuguese King Sebastián.

Portugal

Portugal and Spain, the only two countries in the Iberian Peninsula at the extreme western end of Europe, were one country at the time of the Roman colonization and at the beginning of the period of the Reconquest, which started immediately after the Moorish invasion in the 8th century. Portugal as a name first appears in the Visigoth era, when it was given to a new episcopal city which stood at the point where the road from Lisbon to Braga crossed the Duero river.

Henry of Burgundy became the first Count of Portugal in 1095, after he had been called in from France to help the Portuguese fight the Moors. He married into an old Portuguese family and his son, Alphonso Henrique was the first crowned King of Portugal. Alphonso Henrique won famous victories at Sao Namede in 1128, which gave Portugal independence from the Spanish province of León, and again at Ourique against the Moors. The Moors were finally driven out in 1249 after the battle of Faro.

Sesimbra.

Belem.

The period of Portugal's expansion and the time of the maritime discoveries was heralded in 1415 by the conquest of Ceuta in Morocco. In search of a sea route to the Indies, so that the spice trade would no longer depend on the cumbersome and expensive overland routes, the Portuguese tried to circumvent Africa and sail south. Madeira was discovered in 1420, the Azores in 1427. Gil Eanes went round Bojador Cape in 1434; Diego Gao reached the mouth of the Congo River in 1482; in 1488, Bartholomew Diaz circumvented the Cape of Storms, later given the name of Cape of Good Hope by the king of Portugal. In 1498, Vasco da Gama reached the Indies and in 1500, Pedro Alvárez Cabral discovered Brazil.

From 1581 to 1640, Portugal was dominated by Spain but the country threw off the Spanish yoke in 1640 and made the Duke of Braganza king under the name of Joao IV.

The country is covered with magnificent castles and fortresses reflecting every style of architecture, Moorish at first, then incorporating all the influences of the time. The castles were designed first to fight against the Moors and later to defend the country against the Spaniards. They continued to be built until the 17th century, when the last citadels were erected to protect the border towns of Elvas and Valença do Minho. These final castles testify to the style of the great French architect Vauban.

The Manueline style, named after Manuel I (reigned: 1495-1521), is characteristic of Portugal, and represents a transition from the Gothic style to that of the Renaissance. Special features include spiral columns and lavish sculpture on large windows, doors and balustrades, where laurel branches mix with sheaves of wheat, acorns,

Obidos.

thistles, ropes, anchors, globes and celestial spheres. A perfect example of this extravagence is the Belem tower on the estuary of the Tajo in Lisbon.

SESIMBRA. Erected on a promontory dominating the coast, Sesimbra was built by the Moors but taken by King Alphonso Henrique in 1165. The walled area rises straight from the rock and is dominated by the keep.

TOWER OF BELEM. The Tower was built right in the middle of the Tajo River by Francisco d'Arruda but the river bed has shifted, and the tower is now on the bank. It is an elegant building, from which a spacious platform juts out, flanked with small towers at the corners. The tower is on five levels, marked from the outside by balconies and highly decorated windows in the Manueline style.

OBIDOS. To the north of Lisbon and 6 miles from the coast, this castle defended a small town of the same name and guarded the coast. When the coastline silted up with alluvial mud from the Abidos river, the castle lost much of its military importance. Built by the Moors and renovated in the 12th and 16th centuries, it is now a *posada* (state-run hotel). A major portion of the Manueline façade from the period of the 16th century alterations has been preserved, containing embellished windows and a main entrance adorned with spheres.

BEJA. An impressive fortress of the 13th century by the arid Alentejon plain. It still preserves a powerful military profile, as the walls, keep and battlemented towers are relatively undamaged.

Beja.

Guadamur.

Spain

Spain was known by the Phoenician and Greek navigators, who founded trading colonies along its Mediterranean coast. It was partially conquered in the 3rd century BC and incorporated into the Roman Empire although it was not dominated completely until Augustus defeated the Cantabrians and Asturians at the beginning of our era.

In the 5th century, Spain was overrun by barbarian tribes from northern Europe and from Italy. The Visigoths settled and formed a kingdom ruled from southern France until the Franks pushed them out. After that, the Visigoths took refuge in their Spanish kingdom and made Toledo their capital, where they were quickly assimilated into the Romanized indigenous population.

The Visigoth supremacy lasted until 711, when the Moors crossed the Strait of Gibraltar and subjugated the entire kingdom in a matter of years, either through force —the battle of Guadalete— or by peaceful domination and the imposing of tribute.

The Visigoth nobles and Cantabrians established a small, independent kingdom in the mountains of Asturias in northern Spain. Clusters of semi-independent mountain communities grew up in the foothills of the Pyrenees, from which the kingdom of Pamplona was formed in the west, while the eastern areas developed into small earldoms dependent on the Carolingian Empire. In time, as the earldoms became independent, they united under the Count of Barcelona.

The growing kingdom of Asturias was intent on beginning the reconquest of the central plateau but began to split apart as it grew. Castille emancipated itself from the tutelage of Asturias-Leon towards the middle of the 10th century. Further regions began to splinter away from the body: Portugal left in the middle of the 12th century, to become an independent kingdom; Navarra was partitioned by its king Sancho III from which Aragon was created. So, by the middle of the 11th century, the Peninsula was fractured into the Christian kingdoms of Portugal, Leon, Castille, Navarra and Aragon, and the county of Barcelona, while the Moors and Berbers, now calling themselves «Andalus» dominated the southern and central areas. The Moorish civilization was far superior to that of the Christians in the north.

The Caliphate was dismembered in 1033. When Toledo was conquered in 1085, the new petty Moorish kings feared for their security and solicited help from the Almoravides of North Africa. These new Moslems rapidly dominated the little Moorish kingdoms in Spain and turned to attack the Christians. However, the movement known in Spanish history as the Reconquest, could not be stopped. Saragossa was taken in 1118 by Alphonso I of Aragon, known as the Batallador; the Portuguese reconquered Lisbon in 1147; in the middle of the 13th century, the valley of Guadalquivir fell to Castille, while the Catalan-Aragonese federation took Valencia and Mallorca.

Almohades and Benimerines from Africa came to the help of the Spanish Moslems on two further occasions and the Reconquest was halted but not defeated. The Moors were confined to Granada in the south from 1248 to 1492, where they established their last kingdom, from which the alliance of the Catholic King and Queen, Ferdinand of Aragon and Isabel of Castille, finally drove them. In one sweep, Castille, Aragon and southern Spain were united.

Juana, daughter of Ferdinand and Isabel, married Philip the Handsome of Burgundy, and through the Burgundian inheritance, the Spanish ruled in Europe for more than a century.

MANZANARES EL REAL. The first castle was built on the site by the city of Segovia in the 13th century. The present fortress was commissioned by Iñigo López de Mendoza in 1435. The castle is square, guarded by a sturdy barbican and a large walled enclosure. There is no trace of a drawbridge so it is assumed that access was by means of a ramp through the moat.

GUADAMUR. The military importance of the Toledo region along the Tajo river made it necessary to fortify the banks. It is known that there was a castle at the time of Alfonso VI. This castle was erected by the first Count of Fuensalida in the 15th century, on a rolling hill overlooking the town. The square fortress consists of two large enclosed areas. The outer enclosure is surrounded by a wide ditch and guarded by round towers at the corners. The 80 ft central tower is on the west, reinforced by six smaller towers built into the walls. The castle has been recently restored.

AREVALO. Located at the confluence of the Adaja and Arevalillo rivers, Arevalo castle has two enclosed areas which are juxtaposed; one is square and the other triangular. Next to these is a large central tower with four arched storeys. The castle was originally built into the wall which enclosed the town, but that has now almost completely disappeared. *Arévalo.*

99

JAVIER. This 13th century castle was the birthplace of Francisco Jasso y Azpilicueta, born in 1506, who was cannonized as St Francis Javier. A church was later built to one side of the fortress, diluting the original military use. The castle was completely restored at the beginning of this century.

ALCAZAR DE SEGOVIA. This singular structure stands to the west of the city on a large rock that rises 220 ft above the Eresma and Clamores rivers. An early fortress existed on the site which was the residence of many of the kings of Castille. After the present fortress had been built, it was extensively restored by King Juan II in the 15th century. The defensive elements were taken away to make more space and replaced with weaker ones chosen to please the eye. It was slowly transformed into a stately palace, though nothing could destroy the sharp strategic incline on three sides or the moat cut into the

Javier.

Alcázar de Segóvia.

La Mota.

Molina de Aragón.

isthmus which joins the castle to the mainland.

LA MOTA. The castle guards the city of Medina del Campo which was founded by the Celtic Iberians. After Alphonso VI had taken it from the Moors in 1077 the present fortress was erected on the ruins of the earlier Moorish one. Legend has it that a wealthy peasant, Andres Boca, had the castle built on a small hill close to the city. The central tower was named La Monta because of its great height and it is from this that the castle took its name. Important restoration was undertaken during the reign of John II. Built of brick, the castle consists of an outwork surrounded by a moat and a large walled enclosure; the imposing Monta tower which stands in a corner, is also of brick, reinforced with concrete.

MOLINA DE ARAGON. For a long time, Aragon was a frontier town between the kingdoms of Castille and Aragon. Reconquered in 1129 by Alphonso I of Aragon, the town passed to Alphonso VII of Castille upon the death of the former. Castille's ruler bestowed the town upon the Lara family in perpetuity on the condition that they ensured that the surrounding areas were repopulated.

The present castle is built on the foundations of an earlier Moorish one. The castle is inside a separate enclosure and flanked by eight slender towers. Standing as an outpost higher up the hill is the Tower of Aragon, an impressive octagonal fortified tower linked to the fortress by a long and narrow passage. All that is left of note of the residential quarters are the tall and attractive Gothic windows.

COCA. The site was the birthplace of the emperor Theodosius in 346. The 15th century castle was built by the Fonseca family. The archbishop of Sevilla, Alonso de Fonseca, intended a dual purpose for his castle: impregnable stronghold and sumptuous mansion, and both uses are reflected in the architecture. The edifice is built mostly of brick to a square design. It has two enclosed areas, each overlooked by polygonal towers at the corners. The keep guards the only entrance, which is reinforced by portcullis, look-out posts, thick, heavy doors and machicolation galleries at the top of the tower.

The central fortification has four high, slender, polygonal towers linked by a ramp in the decorative brickwork which characterizes all the exterior structure.

VELEZ BLANCO. Construction of this castle was begun at the beginning of the 16th century by order of the Adelantado Mayor of Murcia, Pedro Fajardo. The style of the hexagonal building is characteristic of the Renaissance: there is a marble courtyard and delicate panelling in the halls depicting scenes from classical mythology. The fine interiors no longer exist. Doors, windows, columns, arcades, statues and panelling were sold to a French collector in 1904, and only the rough exterior is left.

VILLAREJO DE SALVANES. The fortress stands on the outskirts of its town. Only the keep remains, with its three guard posts on each side and the series of simulated machicolation galleries.

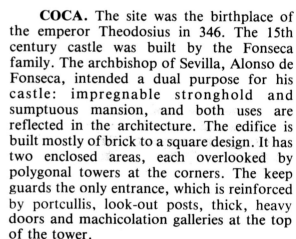

Coca.

Villarejo de Salvanes.

Vélez Blanco.

Ampudia.

AMPUDIA. The first fortress on the little elevation close to the town was a 13th century building, which gave refuge to the rebel Juan Núñez de Lara. The present structure is 15th century. Parts of the exterior courtyard are preserved and the inner yard is complete. There are two large, square towers at each corner of the inner bailey, with the keep to the west. Entry was by means of a drawbridge over the moat and through a gate guarded by high, semi-circular machicolation galleries.

The castle was lost to the «Comuneros» led by Bishop Acuña in 1521 and regained by the Duke of Lerma.

VALENCIA DE DON JUAN. The 15th century castle stands a few yards from the river Esla. The interior has been virtually destroyed but the exterior is still impressive. The main remaining feature is the tall keep reinforced by six rounded guard posts.

Valencia de Don Juan.

SCALIGERO

ITALY
and SAN MARINO

Italy

taly has been inhabited since very early history but its civilization began with the founding of Rome in 753 BC. Little by little, Rome extended its power over the neighbouring villages in the Italian Peninsula, by conquest and by treaty. In 509, the Etruscan kings were expelled and the Roman Republic established.

During the three Punic Wars, which lasted from 264 to 146 BC, Carthage was annihilated, and Rome conquered Sicily, Greece, Macedonia, and the Mediterranean coasts of France and Spain. Augustus put aside the Republic and became the first Emperor. From 473 to 489, the Lombard Odoacer ruled in Italy and Rome's Western Empire ended. The Eastern Empire at Byzantium, under the leadership of Justinian (535-553) reconquered part of the Italian Peninsula.

The Lombards invaded Italy again in 586. Charlemagne, King of the Franks, had himself crowned Emperor of Rome in 800, conquered the Lombards and united Lombardy with his empire.

In the 9th century, the Arabs penetrated into the south of Italy and conquered Sicily. The Hungarians invaded the Po Valley. The Peninsula began to break into small and more or less independent states; the Lombard areas of Benevento, Capue and Salerno became independent duchies, followed by Friul, Tuscany and Spoleto in Marquesados.

The long medieval rivalry between the Ghibelines and the Guelfs took shape. The Ghibelines supported the Germanic Emperor Otto I the Great, while the Guelfs backed the Papacy in the struggle for power. The struggle, which began in 1073, turned to war in 1154 and lost its force with the Hohenstauffen defeat at Tagliacozzo in 1268.

At the end of the 11th century, the

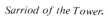

Sarriod of the Tower.

Massa.

Normans settled in the south of Italy, taking Apulia and Calabria from the Byzantines and Sicily from the Arabs. The expansionist policies of the German Emperors of the Hohenstauffen family, and especially the invasions of Frederick I Barbarrossa (1152-1190) and Frederick II (1212-1250), converted Italy into a battlefield. In 1194, Henry VI of Germany led his armies into Sicily and united it with his empire.

The destiny of Sicily was painful and complicated. Under the several times excommunicated Frederick II, the island was yielded to the Papacy, which in turn gave it to Charles of Anjou, brother of the King of France. In 1282, the Sicilians rose against the French and successfully appealed for help to Peter III of Aragón, only to be absorbed into the Aragon holdings.

Venice, Pisa and Genoa (previously Amalfi) became powerful independent republics, basing their power on maritime trade. Silk, brocade, cotton, ivory, porcelain and oriental perfumes were exchanged for goods from Florence, Milan, Flanders and southern Germany. There was constant bickering between the independent republics and finally Genoa gained control of Pisa.

In 1450, Italy was divided into countless little republics, independent lordships and states dependent on other states. Those with a wide territorial base included the Papal States, Milan, Florence, Genoa, Savoy and Venice. The smaller states included Asti, Mantua and Lucca. Lastly, there were a host of entities which consisted of no more than a city and its surrounding area, and among these were San Marino, Parma, Rimini and Regio.

The states formed constantly changing patterns of alliance during the wars which broke out between France and Aragon in 1494, and later between France and Spain. Spain was granted complete power over the Italian Peninsula by the Treaty of Château-Cambrésis in 1559 and retained it until 1793, when Spain's power was assumed by Austria.

Italy built countless castles to repel Arabs and Normans from the south, Lombards in the north, French and Germans. The castles vary as much in the form and style of construction as in the type of materials used. Each of the myriad of Italian states had its castle, and many still survive.

Aci-Treza.

Sant Angelo.

109

THE SCALIGERO BRIDGE. The bridge spans the Adigio river near Castelvecchio in Verona. It was destroyed in the Second World War and what we see now is a reconstruction. A tower stands at each end of the bridge, which is supported by three pillars linked by arcades. The original bridge dated from the rule of the Scaligero family over Verona (1260-1387).

SARRIOD OF THE TOWER. A short distance from Aosta, in the flat part of the valley of Aosta, stands the heavy, predominantly 13th century castle.

MASSE. Originally in the fief of the Malaspina, this 15th and 16th century castle is known as La Rocca. The earlier Tower of the Candeliere, dating from the 13th century, overlooks the city.

ACI TREZA. The Norman castle overlooks a small Sicilian village; out at sea are the Cyclope Islands. According to Homeric legend, it is here that the giant Polyphemus bombarded the ships of Odysseus.

Castel Del Monte.

SANT ANGELO. The castle was built by the Roman Emperor Hadrian in 135 in Rome as a mausoleum for himself and his family, but was converted into a fortress in the 3rd century. For a long time, it was a state prison but now belongs to the Vatican to which it is linked by a passageway.

DEL MONTE. Frederick II of Germany built the castle around 1240. The marble and mosaics which once decorated it and also the water pipes and baths, are a mark of Arab influence. The solid octagonal towers remain intact although the interiors have deteriorated.

LERICI. The 13th century Lerici castle withstood several attacks from the Genoese. It stands on the sea shore overlooking the port.

FENIS. This is one of the best castles in the Aosta valley. Built in 1340 by Aymont de Challant, it was protected by a double enclosure and powerful towers with openings designed for artillery.

SAN TERENZO. The 15th century castle, which overlooks a small fishing village a few miles from La Spezia, has openings adapted for firearms.

Lerici.

Fenis.

San Terenzo.

Estense.

Aymavilles,

Aglie.

ESTENSE. The Estense Castle in Ferrara was built in 1385 and substantially altered on several occasions. Access is by drawbridge.

AYMAVILLES. The 12th century castle, now restored, has the four corner towers preserved intact.

AGLIE. The present building conceals a 12th century castle, built by the San Martino family, beneath its 18th century façade. Charles-Emmanuel III bought it in 1764 from the Marquis of San Martino d'Aglie for his second son, the Duke of Chiablese and totally remodelled it.

Mount Titan.

San Marino

San Marino is the smallest republic in the world. It is only 30 square miles large and has 20,000 inhabitants. Its history began in the 4th century AD when Marino, fleeing from persecution by Diocletian, founded a hermitage on Mount Titan. The community prospered and declared itself a republic in the 9th century. The Middle Ages brought conflict with Hungarians, Arabs and Normans, which the republic survived. It was briefly conquered in 1503 by Caesar Borgia, but since then has resisted absorption by the

surrounding Papal domains and has remained free.

Three massive fortress towers stand at the summit of Mount Titan, linked by a parapet walk: Guaita, Cresta Tower and Montale. Guaita, or La Rocca, is the oldest, dating from the 12th century. It was rebuilt in the 15th century and again in the 17th. The Cresta Tower is from the 13th century and stands at the highest point of the mountain. It is now a museum of armoury. Montale was also built in the 13th century.

THE BALKANS

The Balkan countries are those grouped in the area bounded by the Hungarian plains to the north, the Mediterranean to the south, the Black Sea to the east and the Adriatic Sea to the west. They include Greece, Bulgaria, Albania, Yugoslavia, the European half of Turkey, and Rumania (although Rumania is not fully within the Balkan Peninsula, it shares a common history with its Balkan neighbours).

The region is mountainous, and crossed by the river Danube from west to east. It has always been the ground on which many races and cultures have converted. The first known were the Achaeans followed by the Dorians. The native inhabitants, Ilyrians and Thracians were suppressed. but from the Dorian settlements arose the great Greek civilization.

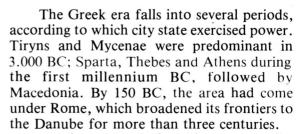

The Greek era falls into several periods, according to which city state exercised power. Tiryns and Mycenae were predominant in 3.000 BC; Sparta, Thebes and Athens during the first millennium BC, followed by Macedonia. By 150 BC, the area had come under Rome, which broadened its frontiers to the Danube for more than three centuries.

At the end of the 4th century, the Balkans were incorporated into the Byzantine Empire, which remained in control until the beginning of the 14th century. Constantinople's power was more and more under threat during the last centuries of the empire, and it lost control of the Balkans before the city itself fell to the Turks in 1453. The Turks absorbed the Balkans, which were not granted independence until the 19th century, when the Turkish empire in its turn had grown lazy and weak.

Veliko Tarnovo.

Veliko Tarnovo, church.

Bulgaria

Bulgaria is entirely mountainous and its history has been marked by its isolation and lack of communications. At the time of the Turkish invasions, the Bulgarians were too scattered in their mountain ranges to be able to unite and resist, but equally they were too dispersed in hostile terrain ever to be completely subdued.

Homer referred to the Thracians, the early inhabitants, in the *Illiad* and the *Odyssey*. The Romans occupied the area in 46 AD and incorporated it into their empire, and it later passed to Byzantium. As Slav tribes penetrated Bulgaria, control slipped away from Constantinople and in the 17th century, the first Bulgarian kingdom was created out of part of present-day Bulgaria, Rumania and southern Russia. The kingdom was at its height under Kufrat and his son Asparub in the 7th century but was destroyed by the Khazars shortly after.

One group of Bulgarians founded a new kingdom along the Danube; another formed the Bulgarian state of Volga which the Mongols erased from the map in the 13th century. The kingdom on the Danube, based on

Cherven.

its capital at Pliska, came to rival Byzantium under Justinian. The Bulgars besieged Byzantium in 711, 811 and 894, and took control of Greece and Transylvania. They were finally repulsed by the Byzantine emperor Basil II in 1014 and the kingdom on the Danube stayed within Byzantium until 1186, when the second Bulgarian kingdom was founded.

The second kingdom was based on the capital of Tarnovo. At the height of its military glory, it extended as far as the Adriatic Sea. Finally dismembered by strong separatist tendencies from within, it was conquered by Serbia in 1386 and annexed to the Ottoman Empire in 1396. It remained a province of the Turks until it regained its independence in 1878.

VELIKO TARNOVO. The fortress of

Veliko Tarnovo dominates the old city, the capital of Bulgaria's second kingdom, from a triangular-shaped promontory on an isthmus in the Janlva River. Access was almost impossible, as it was blocked by three doors (now reconstructed) and a drawbridge. The royal palace, which was principally used by Ivan Asen II, is within the fortress. The Balduin Tower on the summit of the promontory was built in memory of the Latin Emperor Balduin of Flanders, who was taken prisoner at the Battle of Kajolan in 1205. The best preserved of the buildings is the 12th-13th century church.

CHERVEN. The fortress guards the nearby town of Cherven, an important administrative and cultural centre for the Ruse District during the second Bulgarian empire.

Nauplia.

Greece

Greece is a country of mountains, sea, inlets and innumerable islands, and its political development was shaped, even in the earliest times, by its geography. The series of isolated city states which arose, looked to the sea for expansion and trade.

The earliest known settlements are at Tiryns and Mycenea about 3,000 years before Christ. The Minoan supremacy of the Aegean was between 2300 and 1400 BC. The Achaeans invaded from the north about 1270 BC, and were soon actively involved in maritime trade with the Phoenicians and Egypt. They destroyed the Minoan culture of Crete, and razed the city of Troy, during one of many wars in Asia Minor.

The next invasion was by the Dorians around the 8th century BC, from whom came the great classical culture of ancient Greece in the 6th to the 3rd centuries BC. The supreme city states of Athens, Sparta and Thebes developed their democracies and cultures against a background of continuous infighting, which they set aside during the victorious wars against the Persians, before again turning against one another and progressively growing weaker. The vacuum was filled by the new kingdom of Macedonia, which dominated the old city states and acquired a far-flung and short-lived empire under Alexander the Great.

Ancient Greece fell in the 3rd century BC, when it was incorporated into the Roman Empire but it re-emerged with the Byzantine Empire, after the Roman Empire had split into two centres of power: Rome and Constantinople.

The history of Byzantium is one continous struggle, first against invading Huns and Slavs from the north, then against the Arabs moving in from the south, and finally against the Turks, who absorbed the old empire piecemeal before laying siege to Constantinople, which fell in 1453. The Turks took the city as their capital and renamed it Istanbul, and from there they set out to expand into the Balkans, the Hungarian plains and Rumania; and in Asia, into Egypt, Persia and territories as distant as Algeria and Tunisia. The peak of glory of the Turkish Ottoman Empire was in 1566, but its long decline lasted until the 19th century, releasing Greece as an independent state only in 1830.

White tower of Thessalonica.

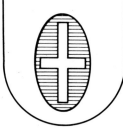

NAUPLIA. Built in the middle of a bay, Nauplia is a small port defended by the fortresses of the Acropolis and the Palameda. Palameda stands on a large rock that rises 550 ft above the sea and is reached by scaling 845 steps on the side facing the old part of the city.

THESSALONICA. Thessalonica was a fortress city before the Turks, who restored the fortifications when they conquered the city. The courtyard and two towers still stand. One of the towers was built by the Christians, and is called the White Tower; the other was Turkish.

Suceava.

Rumania

Rumania is a Latin country in a Slav world. It was conquered by the Roman Emperor Trajan in 106 and remained in the Empire until 271. Although the period of Latin domination was short, the conquerors left their language as the basis of modern Rumanian. During the 4th and 6th centuries, the country experienced a succession of invasions by Goths, Huns, Avars, Hungarians and Lombards, but it was the influence of Byzantium that was felt most.

Hungarians gradually displaced the Byzantines and towards the end of the 14th century, Moldavia and Wallachia became independent principalities, soon to be absorbed within the Ottoman Empire, Wallachia in 1394 and Moldavia in 1512. Transylvania became an independent principality upon the disintegration of the Hungarian kingdom. The three states were federated in 1600, but this lasted only a few years. Finally, at the end of the 17th century, Austria annexed Transylvania and the Turks allowed Moldavia and Wallachia to become dependent kingdoms. Rumania became independent in 1878.

SUCEAVA. While a permanent settlement existed here by the Suceava river in the 7th century, it is in the 14th century that the *Voivoda* Petru Musat I constructed the citadel for protection against the invading Tartars. It was later enlarged by Stephen the Great. The castle itself is from an earlier date. It is a sturdy construction of stone with

Dragomirna.

square towers at the corners, surrounded by a large enclosure buttressed by round towers, which dates from the time of Stephen the Great.

DRAGOMIRNA. This fortified monastery stands in the midst of tree-covered hills. It was built at the beginning of the 17th century, when the Turkish threat was everywhere. The walls of the monastery are covered with paintings and miniatures still in a perfect state of conservation.

Bodrum.

Turkey

The bulk of modern Turkey is in Asia but the small portion on the European side of the Bosphorus is of great importance to any history of Europe or European castles. The ancient Greek colony of Byzantium became Constantinople in the year 330 and then became the capital of the Eastern Empire. The city's walls repelled waves of invaders, including Persians, Avars, Arabs, Slavs and Bulgarians. As from 1071, when the Seljuk Turks won the important victory of Manzikert against the Byzantine Emperor Romanus IV Diogenes in Anatolia, the main threat against the Byzantine Greeks were the Turks.

In 1301, Osman I founded the Ottoman Empire, which lasted until the 19th century. After a major defeat at Ankara in 1402, the Turks reorganised, moving against the Byzantine territories and conquering them until they finally brought down Constantinople in 1453. Selim I subjugated Syria, Arabia and Egypt, and under his successor Suleyman the Magnificent (reigned: 1520 to 1566) the Turkish empire reached its zenith,

after he had added to it Hungary in Europe and Persia in Asia.

BODRUM. Facing the Island of Rhodes, the castle-fortress of Bodrum was built by the Order of Hospitallers in 1402 after the Turks had taken the port of Smyrna (Izmir). Its defences were strengthened in 1480 and 1522 but it was taken by the Turks in 1523 when they invaded Rhodes.

ANAMUR. Located on the Anatolian coast between two sand banks, the castle was built in 1230 by the Karaman Sultans. The exterior courtyard is well-preserved but the living quarters have all but disappeared.

RUMELI HISAR. Built to guard the Bosphorus Straits by Mehmet II, the Conqueror (reigned: 1451 to 1481) so as to support his offensive against Constantinople. Rumeli Hisar, which is on the European side of the Straits, faces Anadolu Hisar on the Asian side, and between them, they dominate the narrowest stretch of the Bosphorus (1,800 ft).

Anamur.

Rumeli Hisar.

Yugoslavia

Yugoslavia was created in 1918 out of the independent nations of Serbia, Montenegro, Bosnia, Croatia, Slovenia and Macedonia. It includes four languages, three religions and two alphabets. The principal nation during the Middle Ages was Serbia, which was a powerful state in the 14th century before it was destroyed by the Seljuk Turks at Kossovo in 1389. It became a dependent state of Turkey in 1396 and was fully incorporated into the Ottoman Empire in 1459. The Serbian state was restored at the end of the 19th century.

Croatia developed into a state in the 10th

century, and carried on incessant wars with the State of Venice and Hungary. It was linked to Hungary by marriage in 1102 and was later conquered by the Turks.

For a long time, the Dalmatian coast was ruled by Venice. Ragusa (Dubrovnik) was an independent republic for a short time, only to be annexed by Turkey in the 15th century. Both Herzegovina and Montenegro, which were more or less independent states, fell to the Turks, Herzegovina in 1415 and Montenegro in 1499.

Mostar.

Ljubljana.

Dubrovnik.

MOSTAR. Mostar means «old bridge». The name refers to the bridge built by the Turks nearly four centuries ago, whose one arch spans the shores of the Neretva river. The castle which guarded access to the bridge is built alongside.

LJUBLJANA. The city, capital of Slovenia, stands on a small hill. The remains of a 15th century castle are still visible.

DUBROVNIK. Once known as Ragusa and an independent republic, Dubrovnik was the main rival with Venice for domination of the Adriatic Sea. It was granted the right to trade with the Infidel by the Pope. Once conquered by the Turks, it was not to be free again until 1718. The city occupies a small peninsula. A large section of the ancient walls still stands and a substantial part of the castle remains.

Contents